TRUMP

GOD'S CHOSEN SERVANT

FOR SUCH A TIME AS THIS...

CINDY ROBERTSON HALL

WORD & SPIRIT
PUBLISHING

Trump, God's Chosen Servant
ISBN: 978-1-949106-39-8
Copyright © 2020 by Cindy Robertson Hall

Published by Word & Spirit Publishing
P.O. Box 701403
Tulsa, OK 74170
wordandspiritpublishing.com

Printed in the United States of America.

The first word that comes to mind to describe this book is *TIMELY*. There could never be a better time to get this message out. Some would say that this book is controversial, but I say it's a prophetic, righteous cry for revival and for Christians to wake up. As I read this book, a passion and love for my country began to grow. And as you read these pages, I believe the same will happen to you. You will burn with courage to fight for righteousness and pray for your country like never before. You will be encouraged to know that your voice must be heard to bring unity and make America great again. This book beautifully depicts that we as a nation must submit to God, the highest authority, and respect the leaders that He appoints over us. I was captivated by this book; it strengthened me both intellectually and spiritually. I know it will do the same for you. Get ready for this book to change you and cause you to grow.

–Philip Renner
Founder of Philip Renner Ministries,
Tulsa, Oklahoma
Missionary/International evangelist/
Author/Award-winning songwriter

CONTENTS

Introduction

Do not speak in the hearing of a fool,
for he will despise the wisdom of your words.
PROVERBS 23:9 NKJV

The mere mention of President Trump's name sends the radical left into orbit, and could even incite a riot. His name either produces feelings of affection from his many loyalists, or hostility from those who oppose him. The mention of collusion or impeachment infuriates both sides—liberals and conservatives—but for vastly different reasons. Mentioning words such as *entitlements, reparations, illegals,* and *diversity* also is bound to evoke feelings of either euphoria or uneasiness. Buzzwords such as *tolerance* and *inclusion* will often elicit the opposite feelings of exuberance or trepidation from individuals, depending on how these words are being applied in a given situation.

New words or phrases are being catalogued almost daily in the far-left dictionary by liberals and the radical left, and the definitions of some words are revised to accommodate their ever-evolving ideology. One of the latest phrases created by radical feminists is "wife guys." To them, a husband who loves and respects his wife is undesirable and a thing to be ridiculed. I'm proud to announce that my husband is a "wife guy" and I'm a "husband gal." We like it that way. The Bible says we're entitled to love and respect each other. Now, that's the kind of entitlement I can agree with!

It seems almost an entire generation, or perhaps individuals from several generations, feel entitled nowadays. This wouldn't have even entered the minds of our founding fathers, or most of the folks they governed. But today, many people feel entitled, whether they've earned it or not, to things that other citizens have worked for and earned. They feel entitled to free stuff, such as welfare, subsidized housing, food stamps, and free health care—even for illegals. Free college tuition has also been added to the growing list of entitlements. Socialist-indoctrinated students are overjoyed at the prospect of attending college for free, or having all their student-loan debt forgiven. It also thrills Democrat politicians, because it gives them a fairly large base of naïve people to whom they can pander. It is incredible how many people accept the concept that things should be free. This may come as a big surprise to some folks, but nothing of substantial value is ever free. You either pay now or pay later; you and future generations of taxpayers pay later—and pay for a long time. Entitlements come with a big price tag; they're never actually free.

One entitlement frequently promoted by radical politicians is reparations for African Americans. No one asks how reparations would be administered and to whom, how the funds would be collected and from whom, and how much compensation should be paid. Nor does the question arise, why stop with African Americans? Shouldn't Native Americans also be entitled to reparations; whose land is it, anyway? Nor do these politicians consider providing compensation to Jews, who've been the most persecuted, enslaved, and mistreated people group on the planet. What about them? And how about other ethnic groups discriminated against during World War II or when first arriving in America; aren't they also entitled to something? Apparently, reparations activists regard only one ethnic group's exploitation worthy of consideration; all other grievances are conveniently ignored.

I once met a very angry political activist who was fully on-board with reparations. He informed me that all white people, regardless of ability to pay, should be required to set up savings accounts for black Americans. I asked him if we should be required to pay reparations to wealthy black billionaires, and his answer was unequivocally—yes! I also asked him about paying reparations to Native Americans, Asians, and Jews, but he was totally opposed to compensating anyone other than blacks. He felt other ethnic groups didn't deserve compensation, because their mistreatment didn't rise to an appropriate level for requiring reparations. The exploitation of Native Americans, Asians, Jews, or other people groups was pure fiction, according to him. I told him that although slavery was a horrific blemish on our country's history, many blacks are now faring much better today in the United States than they would have otherwise fared living in Africa. I also told him that I didn't intend to offend anyone, but black millionaires and billionaires could be living in a little hut in Africa instead of enjoying the luxuries of a palace in America. I further tried to explain to him the biblical concept that what the enemy intended for evil, God will ultimately use for our good. This postulation was extremely offensive to him, and he remained adamant that all blacks, regardless of their wealth and good fortune, deserved reparations.

Now to a key issue that annoys virtually everyone—illegal immigration. Most conservatives have a problem with people crossing our southern border illegally. There are a myriad of reasons for this. First, these people are breaking the law. Why have laws, if they're ignored and broken? Also, a lot of illegals seek asylum in our country based on invalid and false claims—often even falsely posing as family units. Additionally, illegal crossings increase the opportunities for criminals to import drugs, and they allow gang members, sex traffickers, and perhaps terrorists into the country. Further, illegals cost American taxpayers an immense amount of money in welfare, health care, and court costs. They also pose a grave risk to our national security and to individual safety—just ask anyone who has lost loved ones at the hands of criminal illegal immigrants. The cost in the loss of innocent lives is heartbreaking, and the financial burden of prosecuting perpetrators is staggering. Illegal immigration must be stopped for our country to survive as a thriving nation. This is the rational position of most conservative politicians. Not so with radical Democrats; they want open borders and for us to call no one "illegal." The absolute best quote I've ever heard relating to open borders comes from a radio and TV personality named Frank Haley, cohost of *Coffee and Conversation* in Albuquerque, New Mexico. Frank stated, *"Heaven has a wall, a gate, and a strict immigration policy. Hell has open borders!"*[1]

Politicians vying for open borders don't fool most of us, because their real motivation isn't compassion; it's political. Democrat politicians are courting the illegal vote. It matters not to them that noncitizens vote in our elections; in fact, they actually encourage it!

Far-left radicals and liberals of all stripes claim we ought to openly embrace illegals to allow for more diversity in our culture. The United States is already the most diverse country on earth, welcoming immigrants from all ethnic groups. I was amazed when visiting New York City to see people from virtually every country in the world—lots and lots of diversity. Diversity can be both good and bad, desirable and undesirable. While we should welcome some diversity, too much diversity may lead to conflict and serious issues best left in the immigrants' own countries.

Further, some immigrants either are unable or unwilling to assimilate into our society, because there is no commonality with our culture. Their cultures and views are too incompatible and contrasting to successfully coalesce with those of the rest of the population. Honest experts tell us that opposite worldviews and beliefs don't work very well in long-term relationships.

Supposedly opposites attract, and that may be true for a lot of individuals. However, extreme diversity and totally opposite viewpoints do not work very well in marriages, much less in countries. Generally, more problems exist in marriages where couples are more diverse in their social philosophies, religious theologies, and political ideologies. Marriages function much more smoothly when couples are essentially the flipside of the same coin, so to speak. The same is true of countries. Less diverse people groups tend to experience fewer problems. The more diverse a country's population, usually the more issues there will be to confront and overcome.

Also, the more diverse a country is, the more tolerant and inclusive individuals must be in their attitudes toward others. This is not a problem in itself, but it becomes a problem when people assign different definitions to words such as tolerance and inclusion. To apply the proper context to these words, *tolerance* and *inclusion* must not violate the law of man or the law of God. For example, we cannot allow Sharia law in our country, nor should we legalize child marriage, marriage to one's pets or inanimate objects, multiple marriages, or other immoral actions. This doesn't represent tolerance and open-mindedness, but clearly is morally wrong.

Far-left radicals are always calling for more tolerance, but they're the most intolerant people on the planet. They're very exclusive of anyone who does not agree with their points of view. Intolerant radicals especially despise anything Trump—him, his family, those in his administration, and his supporters. What they don't seem to realize, though, is that all those uncivil attacks on President Trump only help to drive his base more deeply into his arms! What they also don't recognize is that the more far left they move, the more voters are waking up and deserting the Democrat Party. There's no need to worry, though; they still have all those illegal voters! Democrat Party loyalists have seduced a large segment of the population into their camp comprised of individuals either too ill-informed or too gullible to understand what they're actually voting for—and the Democrats want to keep it that way! Some voters have sold their souls for a morsel of bread and other free stuff, subjugating themselves to the fatal policies of a destructive political party.

If you find yourself among those in this dismal ditch, buy a shovel and dig your way out! Stop voting for radical Democrats and liberal Republicans who do not have your best interests in mind, who are enamored with themselves, and who are determined to destroy us and our country. Begin supporting and voting for conservative candidates whom you can trust to promote godly values, who have no hidden agenda, and who won't sanction subversive, unpatriotic propaganda. Enough already! Stop listening to liberal rhetoric and succumbing to radical brainwashing! U.S. citizens should be better and wiser than that.

Conservative Christians, in particular, need to stop being captivated and brainwashed by radicals who don't share their values and beliefs. And conservative parents should warn their children frequently about the negative effects of indoctrination and brainwashing by liberal teachers, professors, journalists, entertainers, and politicians. Parents also should use caution when sending their children to secular colleges and universities. They may be sending a conservative youth into a lions' den of liberalism, and get back a young adult whom they no longer recognize. Conservative parents, and all conservatives in general, need to expose the nauseating bait radicals use to trap unsuspecting prey. There are many adults trapped in hopeless lifestyles engineered by toxic politicians, and our nation's youth are at risk of falling into the same quagmire.

Particularly, in major cities, people vote year after year for the same progressive politicians who seemingly have committed their whole political careers to enslaving individuals to despair and hopelessness, while continually promising them a brighter tomorrow. Unsophisticated voters are convinced every election cycle by savvy candidates to continue supporting destructive policies designed to harm them. These individuals remind me of the people of ancient Nineveh who couldn't discern their right hand from their left, until the prophet Jonah was sent by God to show them the error of their ways.

It is very disheartening to see so many people, especially minorities, trapped in *delusional hopefulness.* I'm encouraged, though, to see some of our youth enlightening people to a better path, by asking them to abandon the disastrous Democrat Party. I'm particularly impressed with the Brandon Straka (Walkaway Campaign) and Candace Owens (Blexit) movements. Three other young conservatives providing renewed hope for America are Terrence K. Williams (social media sensation, commentator, and Deplorables Tour comedian), Dylan Wheeler (social media personality and founder of Educating Liberals), and Charlie Kirk (founder of Turning Point USA), and there are many others.

Included in the group of many others is the unforgettable team of Diamond & Silk (political activists, larger-than-life social media personalities, creators of Chit Chat Tours, and former Fox Nation TV hosts). Interestingly, some of these conservatives were former liberal Democrats. I'm so grateful these patriots are now Trump supporters, and playing on the conservative team. I applaud their courageous and meaningful efforts to educate people about the many dangers of liberalism and the unprincipled Democrat Party. Each of them, like a modern-day Jonah, has been sent by God to expose lies and present truth to a confused and deceived electorate.

Naturally, the intolerant radical left despises and opposes these courageous folks. The left is particularly hostile to people like Brandon and Candace. According to radicals, neither of them (a gay male and a black female) are supposed to be independent thinkers or support conservative politics. By virtue of his sexual orientation and her racial identity, they're both in the wrong camp—and they aren't supposed to think for themselves! While they're loved and treasured by conservatives, they have to endure vehement hostility from the intolerant left. Again, I'm so grateful that we are on the same team! Young people such as these give many of us hope for America. Let's help them help other conservatives reelect President Trump in 2020!

I know, I know, the mention of reelecting President Trump might incite some leftists to violence. Something that should provoke conservatives—not to violence—to peaceful but angry protests is the false narrative by radicals about collusion and obstruction of justice, and other spurious impeachable offenses concocted in the perverse minds of ungodly individuals. These untrustworthy people know they're lying, but they lie anyway, hoping they can mislead a gullible public.

Democrats know they've been disingenuous about Trump's involvement in Russian collusion or any criminality warranting impeachment. They also are disingenuous about compassion for minorities, and they're disingenuous about being tolerant and inclusive. Come to think of it, radical Democrats appear to be disingenuous about virtually everything, and they're always in a state of heightened hysteria. They seem to remain in a constant, exaggerated state of fear, anxiety, anger, hostility, and panic. Their fear, anxiety, and panic appear to be real; their hostility and anger certainly are authentic.

Radicals attempt to keep everyone in a heightened state of anxiety—run for cover; the sky is falling! They envision danger where none exists, see racism where none exists, and imagine political crimes where none exist, because they live in a distorted reality. The Bible says in Proverbs 28:1 that the wicked flee when no one is pursuing them.

My hope is that liberals and far-left radicals will wake up, stop the tumult and fearmongering, discern the truth, and divorce themselves from liberalism and extremism. Truth is a hard sell for liberals, and it might be an impossibility for radicals, because their view of reality is so distorted. They vehemently oppose hearing or accepting genuine truth. While conservatives love truth and are truth defenders, radicals and most liberals are truth deniers who find truth offensive. Even absolute facts are denied vigorously and found to be offensive when the facts don't fit their ideology.

Liberals and far-left radicals may be offended by the truths contained in this book, but I encourage them to read it anyway from cover to cover. They might learn something and thank me later. I realize that by writing this book, I may open myself up to all kinds of criticism and scorn from people on the left. Some no doubt will attack me viciously and try to marginalize me. But I believe I've received a mandate from God to tell people the truth, whether they like it or not. Then it's up to each individual to either accept or reject the truth the Lord wants to share with them. Sometimes the truth can be brutal, and sometimes it hurts, but absolute truth should be the pursuit of every individual. My goal in writing this book first and foremost is to be obedient to my Lord and Savior, and also to present the truth as clearly and honestly as possible. Most of this book was written with the divine guidance of the Holy Spirit. If you have any issues with its contents, take your complaints up with the Almighty.

It is my sincere hope that the truths presented in this book will be accepted by most readers, and that those who don't know Jesus Christ will repent and receive Him as Lord and Savior. Some

Christians may feel a need to repent as well for their disobedience to God. I believe the primary purpose of the book is twofold: First, it's evangelistic in nature, to show people Jesus and lead them to Christ; and second, its purpose is to expose the dangers of radical ideology. The intent is to shake Christians and other individuals awake to see the tremendous danger of supporting the Democrat Party. I pray that, once awakened, people will also alert others to the dangers of radical liberalism.

All conservatives and Christians should be exposing the threat that the policies of radicals pose to our country, and asking people to quickly walk away from the Democrat Party. Many Christians in our country have been slumbering for too long; it is past time for them to wake up and take aggressive action to reverse the traumatic injuries they've allowed to be inflicted upon our nation and upon our Christian values. To rapidly improve things in both the spiritual and the natural realms, *all* Christians and conservatives need to wake up—*quickly*. My plea is to wake up, to shake others awake, before it's too late to save the country and our Christian heritage.

If people find themselves deeply offended by the contents of this book, they need to take a closer look at their moral values and beliefs, and allow the Lord to examine the motives of their hearts. This particularly applies to individuals who consider themselves to be believers in Christ. Each of us must determine with certainty whether we are in the faith. This book presents wisdom to those willing to receive it. How individuals respond to the contents of this book will determine whether they are wise, or whether they are foolish. Like the five wise and five foolish virgins described in Matthew 25, people decide whether to be wise or foolish. If individuals find themselves in the foolish category, they can become wise by pursuing truth. In order to pursue truth and become truly wise, people must humble themselves before the Lord, repent of their sins, turn from meaningless theories propagated by man, and accept the wisdom found in the Word of God.

The Lord tells us throughout the Scriptures how to acquire wisdom and knowledge. For people to possess godly knowledge and to gain true wisdom, they must know the Lord Jesus Christ. Proverbs 1:7 says, "The fear of the LORD is the beginning of knowledge, but fools despise wisdom and instruction." Fear of the Lord simply means reverencing the Lord and showing Him proper respect, but this cannot be accomplished without first knowing Jesus Christ as one's Savior. Proverbs 4:7 further states, "Wisdom is the principal thing; therefore, get wisdom. And in all your getting, get understanding." And Proverbs 2:1–5 says, "If you receive my words and treasure my commands within you, so that you incline your ear to wisdom, and apply your heart to understanding; yes, if you cry out for discernment, and lift up your voice for understanding, if you seek her as silver, and search for her as for hidden treasures; then you will understand the fear of the LORD, and find the knowledge of God." The Bible is clear that *true* wisdom, knowledge, and proper understanding cannot be attained without first knowing and respecting the Lord, but most individuals unfortunately try to acquire wisdom from other sources.

Most people view wisdom through incorrect lenses and try to gain knowledge through secular methods. They consider themselves wise, because of their worldly knowledge and their academic degrees. Unless these people are willing to humble themselves before the Lord, they remain without true wisdom and never possess the knowledge God desires to give them. I've heard John Maxwell, a very successful Christian businessman and highly sought-after lecturer, say that everything he teaches comes directly from the Bible. People are awed by his clever business skills and astute knowledge, and often ask him how he has acquired such astounding wisdom. Mr. Maxwell routinely says, "You really don't want to know." Invariably, people insist that they really *do* want to know how he has attained such great knowledge, then he tells them that everything he has just taught them comes strictly from wisdom and knowledge contained in the Bible!

To be truly skilled and knowledgeable, one's wisdom must be based on the Word of God. Have you ever noticed how many people identified as experts in politics, law, academia, science, and the media—to name only a few professions—often appear totally inept or incoherent in their declared areas of expertise? If you're like me, you've surely felt at times that you could have responded to questions better than the proclaimed "experts." That is because these experts were expressing an opinion based on worldly wisdom, while you and I were formulating a response based on godly wisdom. Godly wisdom is what matters! I used to watch a brilliant scientist explain the vastness and complexity of the cosmos. The presentation was scholarly and extremely interesting, but there always seemed to be something missing. The program, though cerebral, somehow felt incomplete. I later realized the missing part was the biblical account of the creation story based on sound godly wisdom.

Often, those who lack and reject biblical wisdom promote their own opinions and agendas. This explains how Democrats and Republicans who embrace liberalism have gotten so far off course in their beliefs and ideology.

It's not my intent to offend anyone, but rather it's my desire to educate liberals to the Word of God that leads to truth and ultimately salvation. Perhaps there is hope for some of them to come to the knowledge of truth; it's not God's will for any of them to perish. Likewise, it's not the will of God for liberals or extremists in either political party to oppose truth and godliness, or for them to continue promoting wickedness that leads to the destruction of souls. The Bible says in Psalm 10:4, "The wicked in his proud countenance does not seek God; God is in none of his thoughts." The Bible further states this question in Psalm 10:13, "Why do the wicked renounce God? He has said in his heart, 'You will not require an account.'" In other words, wicked people will not acknowledge God, nor do they believe that He will ever punish them for their sins.

People who promote evil either do not believe in God, or they think they can somehow outsmart Him. But it's foolish to resist or try to outsmart God. Someday every person will have to give an account to the Lord for their actions—or inaction. Even the motives of our hearts will be assessed by the Lord. Our every word and deed will be judged, to include words we should have spoken but didn't speak and deeds we should have done but didn't accomplish. We will answer to the Lord for our actions and our inaction.

One of my favorite quotes comes from the great man of God, Pastor Dietrich Bonhoeffer, who resisted Hitler's madness during World War II. Bonhoeffer said, *"Silence in the face of evil is itself evil: God will not hold us guiltless. Not to speak is to speak. Not to act is to act."*[2] I've tried for years to tell people that inaction is action—not voting is voting for evil to prevail. I just never stated it with as much eloquence or intellectual brevity as Dietrich Bonhoeffer. He was one of the few people in Germany who was brave enough and wise enough to speak up and resist Hitler, though it cost him everything—even his life. Better to act and be a martyr than to do nothing, and later regret remaining silent! Have you ever wondered how many people in Germany saw warning signs of Hitler's depravity, and later regretted ignoring the beckoning call of God to act in wisdom?

Proverbs 1:20–23 tells us that wisdom calls in the streets and public squares to everyone, but the simple (the foolish) won't listen. If people listen when wisdom calls, then the Lord will make known His Word to them—making them wise. Wisdom cries loudly to people, but foolish and ungodly people ignore it and go their own way. The Bible tells us in Isaiah 35:8 that even God's people can act foolishly and be fools—this has never been more evident than in recent elections!—but the Lord rescues His foolish people who wander onto the wrong path. The Bible says in Psalm 25:8, "The LORD is good and does what is right; He shows the proper path to those who go astray" (NLT). God gives wisdom to those who will listen to His voice, and He prevents them from proceeding the wrong way.

The Lord is a faithful guidance counselor, giving wisdom in abundance to all who seek or ask for it. Wisdom is speaking to people reading this book; wisdom is crying loudly for people to abandon liberal ideology and the ungodly Democrat Party. Wisdom is calling from the streets, from rooftops, and from the airwaves for people to see as God sees and to choose a better course for themselves, their families, and our country. Wisdom summons us to pursue God, gain godly knowledge, and view things from God's perspective.

This book is a call to wisdom. It is written to present truth and expose lies. Some may view and criticize my approach as too blunt or harsh in expressing the truth, but I don't apologize for the manner in which I've separated fact from fiction. Like the prophet Jeremiah, I am grieved by the ungodly behavior of many of our citizens—but I also must speak what the Lord has put on my heart to speak to the people. This book is written to present truth for such a time as this. It's my sincere prayer that truth will prevail, prodigals will repent, evil will be renounced, and our country will be restored spiritually once again.

Note: I have used words such as *liberals, progressives, extremists, radicals, leftists, the left,* and *far left* many times interchangeably throughout the book. Some people view *liberal ideology* as less threatening than that of *radicals, leftists, progressives,* or *other far-left extremists,* but essentially the political ideology of liberals eventually leads to the same ditch. I reluctantly use the word *progressives* to describe Democrats, and absolutely refuse to use *democratic* to describe the Democrat Party. There's nothing slightly progressive, except in a negative sense, associated with their progressive agenda, and nothing remotely democratic about the Democrat Party. These terms are misnomers. The word *progressive* means "to make better, to advance or to grow better," which Democrat policies clearly never do. Their policies only make things progressively worse. The word *democratic* refers to a democracy, principles that the Democrats actually oppose. The party is more closely aligned with socialism than any democratic form of government. The party continues to move further and further to the left, with some party leadership readily endorsing radical extremism—while others do so reluctantly. The few remaining moderates in the Democrat Party have a choice to make: They can either move further left, becoming extremists themselves, or abandon the party and join conservatives.

CHAPTER 1

Chosen by God

The LORD does not see as man sees; for man looks at
the outward appearance, but the LORD looks at the heart.
1 Samuel 16:7b nkjv

Clearly, God chose Donald J. Trump to be the forty-fifth president of the United States, while firmly rejecting Hillary Clinton! God spared us from the presidency of Clinton, and He has given us a temporary reprieve from liberal lunacy at the top level of our government. Virtually, every day my husband and I thank God for President Trump, and for the wisdom God has given him in leading our country. There is absolutely no doubt that almighty God chose Trump over Clinton. According to Hillary's definition of *deplorable*, this means that God Himself also is numbered among the *deplorables*. I would rather be in the deplorable camp with the Lord than to be associated with Hillary Clinton's far-left camp, which is bent on destroying our republic and relegating the United States of America to the status of a third-world country.

I became a deplorable and boarded the Trump Train on Day One, and my husband quickly became a Trump supporter after Governor Scott Walker dropped out of the 2016 presidential race. I jumped on the Trump Train immediately, before there even was a Trump Train! After Trump announced his candidacy, I said to my husband, "Let's get on the Trump Train, and ride it all the way to the White House!" To my knowledge, at that time no one had mentioned or generated the slogan "Trump Train." Another slogan I adopted was "I Stand with the Donald!"

I also immediately began to share with friends and family members my support for Donald Trump. I told them that I believed he was God's choice for the presidency. Both friends and family alike told me that I was seriously wrong. Keep in mind this was before any of the debates, campaign speeches, or the primaries. I received more than one tongue-lashing from well-meaning Christians because of my allegiance to Trump, and some folks thought I was absolutely certifiable. One Christian gave me a stern scolding, telling me that God would never choose an ungodly man like Donald Trump to preside over our country. I was told that God has always been in the business of choosing nearly perfect people to fulfill His purposes—and Donald Trump didn't even come close to fulfilling that mandate! (I found this assertion rather surprising, considering the Bible is replete with examples of God choosing and using very flawed individuals to carry out and fulfill His will upon the earth. Flawed people are the only people who exist, so God has no other alternative but to use flawed individuals for fulfilling His purposes.) I also was warned that Christians are so decadent and deceived that all of us were flirting with disaster and possibly a severe chastening from the Lord for supporting Donald Trump. Actually, I received several such admonishments, so it became difficult at times to keep the faith and a happy countenance with so much condemnation and criticism directed at me.

After receiving so much backlash, I did question whether there was something wrong with my spiritual antenna. Could I somehow be mistaken? Yet I sincerely believed I had proper discernment regarding Donald Trump as God's choice. Still I wanted to be absolutely certain. Toward the end of the primaries, I prayed silently but earnestly for the Lord to reveal His will clearly to me, because I never want to be on the wrong side of God. I asked the Lord to reveal His will clearly with the results of the Indiana primary. Both Senator Ted Cruz and Governor John Kasich were still in the race, and they had colluded with each

other to stop Trump at any cost! They both also had pledged not
to drop out of the primary race, no matter what. Senator Cruz had
been endorsed by the governor of Indiana, which made him a
shoo-in to win, but if not him, then Governor Kasich would surely
be the winner. Well, in case any of you have forgotten, that is not
what happened; neither Cruz nor Kasich won. The victor was
Donald Trump, and not only did he win the Indiana primary, but
both Cruz and Kasich quickly announced they were dropping out
of the race, essentially handing the nomination to Trump. The
Lord answered my prayer soundly, along with the prayers of other
Christians who were praying at the time. Of course, most
Christians had thrown their support strongly behind Senator
Cruz, but my husband and I just never felt the inclination to do
that. We were staunch Donald Trump supporters and remained
committed to his candidacy in spite of all the savage attacks from
Democrats, some establishment Republicans, Republicans in
Name Only (RINOs), friends, neighbors, family members, and
the "fake news" media. My resolve to support Trump might have
wavered briefly from receiving so much flak, but I never got off
the Trump Train!

Although I earnestly believed Donald Trump was God's
choice, I never predicted he would win. After all, the odds were
gargantuan, seemingly insurmountable, against him. The polls
said he couldn't win. The media said he couldn't win. Many
friends and neighbors told me that he couldn't win. For Trump to
pull out a win, three things had to happen: First, the will of God
(which is rarely done upon the earth) had to be understood and
obeyed by the electorate. Second, lots and lots of votes had to be
cast by conservatives, many of whom were discouraged by pollsters
and the seemingly overwhelming odds. Third, election officials
had to ensure conniving Democrats wouldn't steal the election.
The odds were daunting, but I also felt certain that a lying spirit
had been allowed by God, sent out into the land to deceive the
Clinton campaign and her supporters, to include potential voters,
liberal pollsters, the media, and the Democratic National
Committee (DNC). (By the way, a lying spirit is a biblical concept.
Once, it was allowed by God to deceive an evil king of Israel. For

further information on this subject, you may want to read 1 Kings 22:20–23 and 2 Chronicles 18:19–22.)

Clearly, the media was owned by Hillary Clinton. I prayed for a lying spirit to infiltrate the media and the Clinton campaign, which would cause Hillary and her team to become overconfident. An overconfident campaign is a campaign ripe for disaster and destined to fail. I also prayed that FBI Director James Comey would do the right thing and refer Hillary for charges, but as we know, that didn't happen. He unjustly and foolishly exonerated her, even though he had no authority to do so; he had to know she was guilty of numerous crimes.

Anyone committed to justice and truth knew then and knows now that Clinton deserves to be prosecuted and to receive prison time. But Director Comey did something surprising when he later indicated there was "new evidence" and he was reopening the investigation into the Hillary Clinton email scandal. When that happened, it was rumored that several states were going to allow people who voted early for Hillary to change their votes, if they were so inclined. James Comey had suddenly gone from choirboy for the Democrat Party to a despised man, at least temporarily. I bet the former director of the FBI is still scratching his head and wondering why he did such an outrageous thing, stating publicly that he was reopening the investigation right before the general election. He might have thought he did it to cover his misdeeds when things were sure to blow up and go south on the FBI's drummed-up Trump-Russian collusion investigation. But I'm relatively certain that almighty God motivated Director Comey to announce he was reopening the investigation into the Clinton email scandal, and this helped breathe new life into the "Make America Great Again" (MAGA) campaign.

Often life truly is stranger than fiction. It is difficult still for many of us to imagine in the United States of America how our top law enforcement agencies, along with the opposing political party, could manufacture such an elaborate hoax as the Trump-Russian collusion chicanery. How could anyone with even a shred of decency fabricate such a fraud on the American people, and then waste millions of dollars investigating the lie—as if it had some merit? This is especially troubling considering all those involved knew that the party concocting the whole crooked scenario was not only guilty of contriving the dirty scheme, but was also guilty of other serious crimes against humanity and the United States of America. It's also more than a bit disconcerting to think about the amount of taxpayer dollars spent on investigating and covering up this diabolical plot against President Trump. But payday is coming someday! It makes one wonder how many of the folks involved in this disgustingly evil hoax will think it was worth it in eternity. Also, how many of the people entangled in the fake whistleblower and revolting impeachment scheme will be laughing when standing before the White Throne Judgment of almighty God? I venture to guess, not one—not a single one! These ungodly plots perpetrated by wicked men and women, no doubt, will look very different to them in eternity when facing an all-knowing, all-seeing God, unless they repent in advance.

Godly patriots in our country are so grateful that these plots to defeat President Trump failed. The evil plots didn't work during the election, and they still don't work now. Even after the Mueller investigation was concluded and President Trump was proven innocent of any wrongdoing, radical Democrats were unwilling to accept the truth; not surprising. They know the truth, but they won't accept the truth. Trump loyalists never believed the collusion hoax, and they saw it for what it was—an evil and elaborate plot to keep Trump from being elected, or if that failed, to derail his presidency and destroy democracy in our country. The impeachment plot to try to remove Trump from office has been yet another radical assault on democracy. In spite of the lies, fiendish plots, intimidation, persecution, and constant resistance from the Democrats and RINOs, President Trump has been instrumental in restoring Christian values and beginning the process of truly making America great again!

The Trump administration has been very effective in representing our interests, and it has a long list of distinguished accomplishments. We can only imagine how much more impressive Trump's list of accomplishments would be without the constant opposition, adversity, resistance, and hostility. This is why so many of us are overwhelmed with gratitude for our president, and we thank God for motivating the voters to place him in office. True conservatives are ecstatic to have been spared from a Hillary Clinton presidency and the certain calamity that would have followed. After all, she did enough damage as secretary of state. Most conservatives didn't believe Hillary had the moral character or temperament to be president of the United States. In fact, she has been compared for many years to Queen Jezebel in the Old Testament (see 1 and 2 Kings). In my opinion, comparing Hillary to Jezebel might be an insult to Jezebel. If Hillary Clinton had been elected, her radical agenda would have finished off what was left intact after the damage of previous liberal administrations—like a mega-storm hitting the United States, striking every state on the same day. The destruction would have been total and final, with no chance of recovery.

Godly patriots know and understand this, and they should never neglect thanking God for the presidency of Donald J. Trump! Christians should pray for our president and his family because they are under intense demonic attack from the left like no other family in the history of our country. Many of us have heard them say that they have big shoulders and can take the barrage of insults directed at them, but we must continually remember them in prayer. We also should pray for Vice President Pence and his family, along with all Trump administration loyalists and their families. Pray that their enemies are soundly defeated. What happens in our country and with our leaders ultimately impacts the entire world.

The Trumps do seem to have strong shoulders, because they've been attacked viciously and without cause, and have not only survived, but they have been gracious about it. The Trumps have endured unrelenting and merciless verbal violence for years now from Democrats and RINOs. Liberals of every stripe from the "fake news" media, academia, sports, the entertainment world, and our government have teamed up against the Trumps and their loyal supporters to try to discourage and discredit them. Some of the president's critics mock and malign him because of his honest tweets and assertive language, but many of his supporters view his honesty and harsh rebukes as part of his charm. President Trump's critics don't understand the deep loyalty of his *deplorable* followers. If you're a Trump loyalist, then you've got to love Trump with his New York style. I believe this is what endears Trump to the Lord, as it does with many of his supporters.

We the people and almighty God needed a strong, resilient leader to guide the United States at this time in history. We were in a difficult place economically, socially, and spiritually. After many destructive years under the previous administrations, our country's foundations were crumbling and all but destroyed. Many people, particularly Christians, were losing hope, and many of us still wonder if our republic can ever be fully restored. But we do know this one thing: God chose the right man for this turbulent time in history. The Lord chose Donald Trump from a long list of Republican and Democrat Party candidates.

When I looked at the seventeen candidates running for president on the Republican ticket, I felt sure that Donald Trump was the only one who could defeat Hillary Clinton—and that he was the one whom God had chosen to do it! I mean no disrespect to the other sixteen candidates, most of whom are very fine individuals. But one by one, I was able to eliminate each of them very quickly. Some of them were too gentle, too kind, and just too doggone sweet. Yes, you heard me right! Some of the candidates were too gentle to shoulder the burdens of being president of the United States. I wouldn't have felt confident with them facing off against obnoxious "fake news" journalists, much less ruthless foreign dictators. Several of the candidates were either far too politically moderate or much too liberal; some were tediously boring; and some of them just weren't ready for prime time. A few of the candidates actually made my husband and me feel nauseous when we heard them speak, and we were happy to see them exit the race. Several candidates weren't conservative enough for anyone except establishment Republicans or RINOs. We really liked former Governor Mike Huckabee's tax plan—he is a great patriot. The only other candidate besides Donald Trump who appealed to me personally was Senator Lindsay Graham. During a couple of debates, he made impassioned pleas about defeating terrorism over there so we don't have to do it over here! At least Senator Graham seemed to understand the gravity of the situation concerning terrorism and protecting our homeland, which was something the Obama administration just never seemed to grasp. But, again, I believed from day one that Donald Trump was the candidate chosen by God to defeat Hillary and begin the process of restoring our nation.

Trump's assertive, sometimes brash, and at times humble New York style appealed to my husband and me, and resonated with many other voters. We realized Trump wouldn't fold up like an accordion at the first sign of trouble. (Lesser men would have resigned by now!) Shrewd voters also recognized what a great plus it was that Trump wasn't an establishment guy, and that the word *politician* didn't appear anywhere on his résumé. On the other hand, some establishment Republicans and the *holier-than-thou club* saw Donald Trump as unqualified and a threat to our republic. President Trump is a threat to dangerous policies and the detestable lies of the Deep State, swamp creatures in Washington, D.C., radical Democrats, RINOs, and the "fake news" media. Trump is a patriotic American and a great friend to other patriots. He shines as a light in a very dark place, exposing the horrific treachery of profane politicians. Radical politicians are a menace to the security of the United States, our way of life, religious liberty, peace, and tranquility.

President Trump was chosen by the all-wise God for such a time as this!

C H A P T E R 2

Dark Menace or Great Friend?

The righteous should choose his friends carefully,
for the way of the wicked leads them astray.
PROVERBS 12:26 NKJV

The Bible advises us in numerous places to choose our friends carefully. We would be wise to follow the same biblical advice when choosing our political leaders. But many people have listened to ungodly rhetoric for so long that it's nearly impossible for them to identify honest, ethical leaders anymore. The dishonesty of many politicians makes it difficult for people to discern fact from fiction. When they hear truth, it frequently sounds fictitious to them and is rejected, but when people hear lies, the lies sound like indisputable facts that should be trusted.

The Bible cautions people to be careful of what they hear and how they hear (Mark 4:24 and Luke 8:18). If people listen to, accept, and repeat lies, then the biblical law of sowing and reaping gets activated. This means that a person who hears, accepts, and repeats lies will continue to accept (reap) more lies as truth, but the individual who accepts truth will understand and receive more truth. Also, people who habitually speak and accept lies eventually will have a difficult time discerning good from evil. They may even convince themselves and others that lies are acceptable. We see

9

this happening today in the media and in the halls of Congress. A few years ago, a U.S. senator was brash enough to stand on the Senate floor bragging about how his lies had destroyed the reputation of another politician. He viewed lying as acceptable behavior. This former senator isn't the only person to believe this way. Many people, particularly politicians, view lying as perfectly acceptable when maligning a political opponent or trying to deceive a gullible electorate.

Voters must learn to choose their political leaders carefully, but the problem with many voters—including Christians—is their inability to distinguish the good guys from the bad guys. This makes them easy prey for dishonest politicians to outwit and lead astray.

It's very disheartening to observe so many voters allowing themselves and our country to be ravaged by extremist politics, because they cannot easily detect friend from foe. I'll state this as emphatically as I possibly can: Radical Democrats and liberal RINOs don't have our best interests in mind, can't be trusted with our welfare, aren't the good guys, and are not our friends! In fact, the greatest threat to our form of government and to *we the people* is now, and always has been, liberalism. We must choose more wisely, because often those who lead us cause us to err and destroy the way of our paths (Isaiah 3:12).

Liberal policies espoused by both radical Democrats and RINOs always manage to lead us to a dark, menacing place. Democrats and their RINO counterparts have a long history of advancing unsound beliefs, but never as flagrantly as today. In previous decades, they were extremely skillful at prevaricating and disguising their destructive policies in order to mislead unsophisticated voters. Also, there was once an era when many of them appeared to be patriots who loved their country, unlike most of them today.

Radical ideologues, most of whom are avowed Democrats, have no fear of being outed as extremists. They *are* extremists! They proudly wear this badge of dishonor with what they view to be distinction. Radical extremists no longer try to conceal their hatred for America, nor do they vaguely attempt to camouflage their dangerous ideology. They are more interested in protecting the *imagined rights* of illegal immigrants than the constitutional rights of U.S. citizens. Radical-left extremists endanger both our national security and our national sovereignty by insisting on open borders, by aiding our enemies with large financial gifts, and by trying to overthrow our duly elected president. Extremists also are now more interested in saving animal and plant life than in saving human life. They eagerly support infanticide and euthanasia, embracing the *death culture* so prevalent in our society today. Their values pose a serious threat to all citizens—not just to conservatives but to radical extremists as well.

Those most vulnerable to the lethal policies of extremists are unborn babies, particularly in inner-city black communities.

A few years ago, I saw two liberal white women on TV discussing the merits of abortion for black women. One of the major benefits, according to them, was the "positive effect" abortion has on the crime rate in inner cities. These ladies stated that crime rates in major cities across the United States would be out-of-control without abortion, so abortion was being touted as a desirable method to combat inner-city crime, especially among blacks. Imagine conservatives saying anything this offensive! A lot of liberals praise the virtues of abortion, but what they don't tell people is just how truly racist it is. Abortion is particularly encouraged in minority communities, so it should come as no surprise that minority babies are aborted at a disproportionately higher rate than white babies. Liberals have been busy for years convincing gullible black women to abort their babies, but it's still murder and racism—sort of a modern-day lynching. Racists appear far less menacing today, though, without their white robes and hoods! The spirit of Margaret Sanger and the KKK is still alive and well in the United States and the radical Democrat Party, yet it seems to go largely unnoticed by a naïve, uninformed public.

It's mystifying to most conservatives that spiritual leaders from minority communities support radical-left politicians and also frequently encourage their congregations to do so as well. Perhaps they're unable to properly discriminate between the good guys and the bad guys, but the truth should be evident, especially to spiritual leaders, that the good guys are pro-life while the bad guys are pro-death.

If you're one of those who has trouble separating truth from fiction and discerning good guys from bad guys, there is an answer to your dilemma. The Lord is currently using radical, liberal, and conservative politicians to amplify the differences in their ideologies, and He is asking people to wake up and walk away from the unprincipled practices of the Democrat Party. The Lord also is guiding people to stop voting for liberals, whether they're Democrats or Republicans. Many decent people have been deceived and bewitched in the past to support radical politicians to their own detriment. Sadly, even some Christians are also bewitched and have foolishly aligned themselves with an ungodly political party opposing Christ and Christianity.

It's time to wake up and take sides: Whose side are you on? As for me and my house, we are on the side of the Lord. People can no longer plead ignorance or claim to be uninformed about the vastly different political views of the two major political parties in the United States, and we no longer have the luxury of not voting. Voting is both a privilege and now a necessity for every conservative, especially for Christians. The Lord is saying to all believers, "I've shown you the way—now walk in it!"

The Lord has drawn a distinct line in the sand, making it easy for anyone who loves truth to separate right from wrong and discern good from evil. The Bible tells us in James 4:17, "To him who knows to do good and does not do it, to him it is sin." All it takes for truth to be suppressed and evil to prevail is for good men to zip their lips, sit on their hands, and do nothing. It's time for all good men and women to rise up, make their voices heard, and ensure their votes are counted on the side of righteousness!

For several years, I have attempted to educate voters about the fatal policies of the Democrat Party. Shrewd people listened, and some even changed their political party affiliation, while others scorned my advice. I tried, unsuccessfully, to persuade some lifelong Democrats not to vote for Obama. Fortunately, others eagerly heeded my advice. For some people, it took eight years of President Clinton and eight years of President Obama for them to finally wake up to the truth. For other voters, it took the Benghazi catastrophe and Hillary's email scandal to ultimately jar them awake. Some staunch Democrats, especially in Red States, believed Hillary was undoubtedly responsible for the deaths of the Americans in Benghazi and for endangering our national security. I believe this sentiment was repeated perhaps all across the United States during the general election in 2016, ensuring Trump the presidency. I also believe the Lord used the prayers of the saints to wake these people up. I sincerely thank all the generals of the faith who prayed so diligently for citizens to wake up and vote wisely during the 2016 presidential election, and who continue to pray for favorable results in 2020. The Lord has even awakened some individuals seemingly in one of the most unlikely places—the LGBTQ community—and they're now able to distinguish good guys from bad guys!

I saw an interview in March 2019 on the *Life, Liberty & Levin* show with Brandon Straka from the LGBTQ community. Brandon is the founder of the Walkaway Campaign from the Democrat Party. I found Brandon to be a very insightful young man and extremely courageous. I don't know if he or any of his supporters will ever read this book, but I would like him to know that I pray for his safety and the safety of those brave enough to walk away from the Democrat Party. It cannot be an easy feat, and it may even be dangerous. We can help Brandon advance the conservative movement by supporting him and donating funds at his website: www.walkawaycampaign.com. To Brandon and his followers, I extend a warm embrace and say, "Welcome aboard the Trump Train; welcome to the often-wimpy, frequently cowardly, but mostly God-fearing Republican Party—and more importantly, to the conservative movement!"

Though better than extremist Democrats, the Republican Party needs a major overhaul to make it a strong, viable party with wider appeal for future generations. First, *everyone* in the Grand Old Party (GOP) needs to unite behind President Trump and support his conservative agenda. Also, GOP members need to stand up against the malicious onslaught of the radical left, not allow themselves to be bullied, and fight for what is right for their constituents, for our president, and for the country. Further, the GOP needs to grasp that true, *dyed-in-the-wool* conservatives can't be easily persuaded to vote for liberal candidates, nor can we be swayed by the lies of "fake news" journalists to relinquish our loyalty to President Trump and the conservative movement.

Republican politicians and conservative journalism outlets should wise up, support their base and encourage others to join them, and stop pandering to liberals and massaging the egos of radicals committed to destroying the United States. (This prompts a very important question: What in the world is happening at FOX News? If it keeps moving in the direction it is going—like other liberal networks—FOX won't have much viewership left. Conservative viewers are dropping FOX News like insects hit with Bug Stop! There are many journalists and commentators now employed at FOX whom a lot of us refuse to watch.) I believe I speak for most conservatives when I make the recommendation to the GOP leadership and to FOX News corporate executives to locate candidates of a higher quality to run for public office, and a better caliber of journalists to represent our points of view. We don't respect and don't want to vote for RINOs, and we don't like to listen to liberal or leftist commentators. By the way, this recommendation should be heeded only if the GOP and FOX executives want to stay in the business of genuine conservatism. Get a revelation: True conservatives won't listen to or support Trump bashers—period!

Trump haters employed at FOX or elsewhere are not our friends! But our earnest plea to them and to radical politicians is to wake up, become followers of Christ, and become honest-to-goodness conservatives, or just go away and stop trying to impose their liberal beliefs and undesirable legislation upon us. We don't want free health care, free college tuition, a Green New Deal, socialism, or global warming forced upon us, and we don't hate homosexuals, Jews, or any other minority group. We just want to keep our country and not play identity politics or other dangerous games that divide people—and we don't want any new taxes to pay for all that *free* stuff and their climate change hysteria programs!

Any observant person has realized by now that the theory of global warming has magically become climate change, since the concept of global warming didn't pan out amid all the recent blizzards experienced in so many areas of the country. Climate change is coming one day, and it is bringing with it a truly dreadful outcome. The Bible informs us that when Jesus Christ returns and judgment is meted out, the earth will burn up with fervent heat. Now, *that* is true global warming that will affect every sinner! This should really scare climate change alarmists, but it probably won't. It also should scare those individuals who were engaged in the Russian collusion hoax, the *impeach Trump movement*, and the attempted Kavanaugh takedown, but it probably won't. I hope they repent, but unfortunately, they probably won't.

It's not my intent to offend or be unkind, but it's senseless for individuals to waste time worrying about climate change or incriminating innocent people rather than acknowledging and addressing their own spiritually bankrupt condition. These folks are in a menacing place spiritually, and they need to repent and seek forgiveness to avoid true global warming. Again, it's not my intent to be offensive, but sometimes truth needs to be stern and unapologetic. With some folks, a gentle approach works. But with others, they must be slapped in the face with hard facts. Both of these approaches were used by Jesus to get people's attention. Usually Jesus was extremely gentle, but at other times He verbally slapped people in the snout—this was particularly true when He was addressing ungodly religious leaders. This was the method also used by John the Baptist. He sometimes rebuked people with a fierce scolding. I see the Lord using President Trump as sort of a modern-day John the Baptist wrecking ball. Trump isn't shy about making honest, but often scathing comments about people when he thinks it's necessary. At other times, he's humble and gentle with individuals whom he respects—those who are committed to truth—but he very often uses sharp criticism toward those who distort the facts and are deserving of a good tongue-lashing!

Actually, President Trump and his entire family have been gracious and used more restraint than most people would use in similar circumstances. The barrage of insults and vitriol spewed toward them has been heartless and unrelenting. The vicious attacks by radicals haven't just been insensitive, but absolutely mean spirited and downright cruel. Although the ceaseless assaults from godless people in Congress, Hollywood, the media, and elsewhere have been merciless, I predict President Trump will still come out on top.

Many Christian leaders have compared President Trump to King Cyrus, who is mentioned numerous times in the Bible. His name can be found in several books of the Old Testament, including 2 Chronicles, Isaiah, Ezra, and Daniel. I can see a definite correlation in that President Trump truly has been instrumental in restoring religious liberty in the United States, and *figuratively* decreeing that the temple and walls of Christianity be rebuilt. Christians have been freed from religious persecution and Babylonian captivity—so to speak. I certainly understand Trump's comparison to King Cyrus, but regrettably many Christians have missed the correlation and see President Trump as an enemy. Imagine how foolish Zerubbabel, Ezra, Nehemiah, or other Jews would have been to scoff at King Cyrus and reject his decree to rebuild the Temple in Jerusalem. Yet confused, ungodly citizens of the United States have scoffed at Trump and have tried to overthrow his presidency—some apostate Jews and other godless people claiming to be Christians! These individuals remind me of the scriptures written by Peter and Jude describing people who lack understanding as being like brute beasts. Peter and Jude (a brother of Jesus) were really tough on folks, comparing them to brute beasts for speaking evil about things they didn't understand—sounds similarly descriptive.

Those opposing Trump lack godly wisdom and spiritual discernment. President Trump is being used by God to raise the awareness of people, and Christians in particular, to the dangers of radical-left politics. The spiritual darkness is indeed deep and extremely hazardous when Christians are unable to discern the truth. President Trump is perhaps the greatest friend that people of faith have ever had in the Oval Office. According to the Heritage Foundation, President Trump has a more conservative track record even than that of President Reagan at the same point in his administration.

Unlike those on the left, President Trump has proven to be a wonderful friend and a remarkable leader. He is an incredible friend to minorities, conservatives, Christians, first responders, armed forces personnel, military veterans, the state of Israel, and the United States of America. I urge people to learn to distinguish the good guys from the bad guys. Stop listening to the dark, menacing lies of our foes, and instead accept the friend of truth.

CHAPTER 3

Politics and Religion

The simple believes every word,
but the prudent considers well his steps.
PROVERBS 14:15 NKJV

Some well-meaning theologians and other people with good intentions have warned us over many decades, or perhaps centuries, that politics and religion don't mix, but I respectfully disagree. I do, however, agree with these wise quotes made by two distinguished individuals. Pastor and televangelist Jerry Falwell Sr. once said, "The idea that religion and politics don't mix was invented by the devil to keep Christians from running their own country."[3] I would add the concept also was invented by the devil to seduce Christians into voting unwisely and destroying their own country! Theoretical physicist Albert Einstein said, "Those who believe politics and religion do not mix understand neither."[4]

The idea that politics and Christianity don't mix is actually a cunning lie crafted by the adversary to create havoc. Then this lie is unintentionally advanced as truth by deceived individuals. Because many Christians readily accept the big lie about not mixing politics and religion, it has been responsible for causing immeasurable damage to the Christian faith. Voters must come to recognize this cruel lie as fallacy and stop severing their faith from the way they approach politics. They need to reject this crafty lie, along with the clever lies of dishonest politicians.

Voters should never underestimate the lies of calculating politicians and should remember that all their conniving lies aren't equal. Significant lies may gravely harm or destroy people, while minor lies may cause no severe consequences. If dishonest politicians tell voters insignificant lies, people suffer no loss. However, if voters elect deceptive politicians who are lying to them about important issues, the ramifications may be devastating. It's of the utmost importance that individuals know what they're voting for, and it is every voter's responsibility to determine if politicians are being honest or dishonest. Many political candidates claim to be persons of faith who embrace religious liberty, profess they are dedicated to helping the poor and middle class, and insist they are filled to overflowing with compassion for everybody. But many politicians are dishonest and cannot be trusted with our welfare.

Religious liberty can mean very different things to different people, especially to politicians. Some politicians claiming to be Christians believe in religious freedom for every faith except Christianity. Before people endorse candidates, they need to question what politicians mean by "religious liberty" and where they stand on other important issues. Are these politicians *counterfeit converts to the faith,* or do they have an actual history of following Christ and supporting Christianity? When politicians speak of helping the middle class, what group of people are they referring to? What income level do they consider middle class? Also, is the compassion that candidates claim to have authentic or politically motivated? Does their professed compassion only extend to people entering our country illegally, or does it extend to unborn babies and citizens of the United States? If political candidates are running for reelection, what do their voting records reflect? What have they supported or opposed in the past? Are they pro-life or pro-choice? Have they supported liberal or conservative causes? Answers to these and other important questions are essential before Christians should endorse any politician for public office. Yet, a lot of naïve and uninformed voters often are quick to support candidates without knowing anything about their political history or ideology.

Many voters, including Christians, would eagerly vote for the Antichrist as long as he was of their particular political persuasion—a Democrat. This is because many people accept the concept that they should keep politics and their faith separate. They also have bought into another big lie—that if they are minorities, they cannot trust Republicans, and therefore they must be Democrats. This is one of the most insidious lies ever inflicted upon a group of unsuspecting individuals, and it has managed to thoroughly paralyze and immobilize most minority voters. Even if they're social conservatives, they are convinced they have no other alternative but to vote for liberal or far-left Democrats—otherwise they're guilty of being disloyal to their own race. This cannot be an easy position to be in, and it must be very confusing spiritually. Fortunately, some minorities have come to realize they've been lied to, and they are abandoning the Democrat Party. It breaks the hearts of conservatives to see their black and Latino friends trapped by this cruel lie. Conservatives feel completely incapacitated in helping them discern the lie, because Republicans normally are seen as untrustworthy bad guys. Most minorities have bought the big lie, and conservative Republicans are helpless to do anything about it. So, in reality, both Republicans and minorities are held captive by the same vicious lie. A lot of poor whites also have succumbed to this sinister lie, as they've been told that Democrats are *for the poor* and Republicans are *for the rich*. Anyone believing or promoting this lie is either a gullible person or a deceptive liberal. One need only look at how the poor and minorities are faring under the leadership of Democrats, and the number of millionaires and billionaires supporting Democrat candidates, in order to debunk this colossal lie.

Democrat politicians often make a lot of noise about taxing the rich and helping the poor—yet another big lie! But with so many voters buying the lie, it's no surprise that the rich get richer while many minorities and the poor suffer. Progressive politicians cannot be trusted with the financial welfare of poor or middle-class voters.

This reminds me of a story I saw about a family of coal miners in West Virginia who lost their livelihood after President Obama's war on coal. The father lost his job after the coal mine where he worked was shut down; he was having a tough time economically. His son, a college student, was complaining about how the mines being closed essentially destroyed their former lifestyle. He and his dad were staunch Democrats, had voted for Obama, and felt betrayed by his administration. I wondered how anyone could be that gullible. After all, candidate Obama promised to shut down as many coal mines as possible—in order to save the environment. I was flabbergasted that these men didn't realize that a vote for Obama was a vote for an *all-out war* on coal mining. Perhaps they believed Obama wouldn't fulfill his promises and coal mining would be safe. A lot of politicians, unlike President Trump, rarely deliver on their promises. But it should be clear: Any liberal politician promising to close coal mines in order to combat climate change and save the environment can be trusted to do just that! Liberals never lie when proposing radical policies detrimental to the country and our standard of living. They can be trusted to keep promises proving harmful to us, because they're convinced their policies are good for us. This is why so many of them now embrace socialism; they truly believe that socialism is more desirable than capitalism and a democratic or constitutional republic form of government.

Voters, especially Christians, need to be more careful with whom they trust to protect their economic and spiritual welfare, and they must stop voting for radical politicians who oppose their faith and destroy their livelihood. Many of them vote for politicians whose values are diametrically opposed to their own beliefs. It is disconcerting and unconscionable to me the large number of individuals who vote for politicians with whom they sharply disagree. The mistake that Christians sometimes make is to view politics as secular and faith as spiritual, but everything a Christian does is spiritual. Faith and politics should never be severed or seen as unrelated. To do so is to flirt with disaster.

Now, with all the myths relating to politics and Christianity firmly dispelled, there should be no question as to how people of faith should vote. Candidates readily share their political ideologies with voters. Also, the Democrat and Republican Party platforms are easily accessible on the internet for viewing. It's the responsibility of every potential voter to review these platforms from A to Z, beginning with *A* for *Abortion*. The Democrat Party clearly states it is pro-choice and a staunch supporter of Planned Parenthood, while the Republican Party indicates it is pro-life and opposes funding for abortion clinics. Any Christian should be able to make an informed decision based on this *one issue alone* which party to support. No Christian can support the culture of death embraced by the Democrat Party—without grieving God and violating His laws.

Individuals voting for radical Democrats and still opposing President Trump's conservative agenda are in rebellion against God. Many know they're wrong. Even Speaker Pelosi must know the Democrat Party is wrong to be so divisive, but she has been backed into a corner by the radicals in her party. Pelosi may currently hold the gavel, but she no longer holds the power.

Speaker Pelosi and company have manufactured so many lies trying to unseat the president that they have no credibility left. They have learned many of Saul Alinsky's rules for radicals exceedingly well, skillfully implementing rules five and eight particularly. Rule number five states, "Ridicule is man's most potent weapon."[5] Rule number eight says, "Keep the pressure on."[6] Radical Democrats have used these rules rigorously, but have grossly violated rule number seven, which cautions, "A tactic that drags on too long becomes a drag."[7] Their many lies and fiendish plots to destroy President Trump have become a tremendous drag, and fellow citizens are weary of the rage and unscrupulous antics of the Democrat Party, not to mention the tremendous costs to taxpayers associated with their dastardly schemes. The impeachment of an innocent president is rash, diabolical, and profoundly stupid—also criminal—and is sure to backfire politically. All the villainous plots only serve to make the Democrats appear insufferable, while making the president look more and more like a knight in shining armor!

By the way, many conservatives don't believe there was ever a whistleblower associated with the Ukraine phone call. Many people think Congressman Adam Schiff made the whole thing up, that he himself is the imaginary whistleblower. We also believe the Democrat Party and the Deep State know there was no whistleblower—including the Department of Justice Inspector General. With good reason, we no longer trust many of our government leaders.

The abhorrent behavior of Congressional Democrats should be of grave concern to every citizen. The entire Democrat Party has deteriorated to such a level of depravity that it's now clearly irredeemable. This is why Christians, in particular, should walk swiftly away from the Democrat Party. They cannot possibly endorse the corruption of Democrat politicians and oppose Trump's conservative agenda without greatly offending God. Christians validating the actions of radicals are culpable of egregious behavior. Their actions are inexplicable, and the spiritual battle some Christians fail to properly acknowledge and engage in is inexcusable. They fail to recognize that their brazen disobedience has helped cause the mayhem. According to them, President Trump and conservatives are to blame!

CHAPTER 4

The Real Battle

We do not wrestle against flesh and blood,
but against principalities, against powers,
against the rulers of the darkness of this age,
against spiritual hosts of wickedness in the heavenly places.

EPHESIANS 6:12 NKJV

A fierce spiritual battle is raging in the heavenly realm over the United States like never before. This war has been intensifying over the past several decades and is being fought for the very soul of our nation. The adversary is trying to thwart the purposes of almighty God by attempting to overthrow our government and forcibly remove President Trump from power. The enemy is engaged in a political war to defeat conservatism, undermine Christianity, and destroy capitalism by establishing a godless form of government. The enemy is also using radicals to sow rage, distrust, and discord among citizens, deception and rebellion within Christian circles, and strife among political leaders. The real war encompasses both politics and religion.

The spiritual battle has grown more and more intense with each passing year, not just in the United States but also abroad. It's not coincidental that similar attacks by extremists in Israel have been directed toward Prime Minister Benjamin Netanyahu. The adversary desperately wants to create chaos by dismantling conservative governments instituted by God, and there's no lack of deceived individuals, including Christians, willing to assist him. Most Christians recognize a spiritual battle is raging, and many are in the war, but fighting on the wrong side! They have unwittingly aligned themselves with the adversary and radical extremists opposing conservatism and the Lord Jesus Christ.

The Lord warns in the Word of God that enmity will exist between the people of God and the people of Satan; hostility and friction will always be present between the opposing forces of good and evil. Revelation 12:12 also warns that the wrath of the devil will intensify as we advance closer to the end of the age, and the Scriptures indicate deception will be rampant throughout the world during that time frame. A fierce spiritual battle, rooted in deception, has shrouded truth and taken many people captive.

The adversary is using deception and the intense animus of radical politicians and other antagonistic individuals to vent his fury against the people and plans of God. Christians must be thoroughly engaged in the spiritual war being waged against our country and citizens, and we cannot continue electing deceived politicians to be our overseers. Their radical policies will bring about desolation, just like in the past, if they ever gain absolute control of our government. Radicals were manipulated in the past to bring Native Americans to the brink of extinction, adopt slavery, and later impose Jim Crow laws and the segregation of the races. Radicals were also responsible for lynching black citizens and brutally attacking white conservatives who supported civil rights. No sane person does these horrific things without being deceived and guided by evil forces.

Radicals are deceived, and they use deception to victimize other unwary individuals, especially minorities. This is why major cities run by Democrats are in crisis and why many minorities feel incapable of ever aspiring to the American dream. The goal of radical politicians is to keep these people loyal to a political party that needs them to stay in power but has no commitment to help them improve their lives. The objective is not to help minorities up, but to keep the majority of them down, and if possible, poor and uneducated. Helping the *little guy* is just a ruse to keep naïve people in bondage. Welfare and other social programs, invented by radicals to supposedly help minorities, are also just ploys to trap people in dismal dependency.

A devious plan was concocted by President Johnson in the 1960s to keep black Americans indebted to the Democrat Party and essentially, wards of the State. He was evidently opposed to civil rights and intensely disliked African Americans. His administration devised a plan to offer welfare to black citizens in order to gain their loyalty and make them think Johnson and the Democrat Party were their friends. President Johnson even bragged that black people were too ignorant to know they had been scammed! He also seemed to believe his sinister plot would be successful in making blacks feel so indebted to him and the Democrat Party that they would register and vote Democrat *forever*—and he hasn't been far from wrong! Johnson's behavior was crude and incredibly deceitful. But he is the person many black Americans and the Democrat Party credit with granting civil rights to a repressed people, who incidentally would have already enjoyed those rights were it not for the racist policies of the Democrat Party! Truth truly is stranger than fiction. No doubt radical, *self-proclaimed* civil rights leaders are aware of Johnson's history and motivation but choose to ignore it and, therefore, are complicit in helping keep minorities in bondage to the State and wretched despondency. Dr. Martin Luther King Jr. would be appalled at their behavior and acquiescence.

Dr. King's "I Have a Dream" speech will never come to full fruition or be truly realized by many black Americans until they reject radical politics and embrace conservatism. President Trump offers genuine hope and authentic change for minorities, but radicals claim he is a racist and ruining America. This is blatantly false. In reality, it's radical Democrats and their liberal policies that harm minorities. Radicals frequently cry wolf, but they themselves are the wolves! They know that if minorities ever wake up to the devastation caused by their radical ideologies, the Democrat Party will cease to exist. They won't let that happen, unless voters, particularly Christians, unite to deal a death blow to their ungodly party. While Christians still have the opportunity, they need to vote radicals out of office—and replace them with those representing their values and worldview.

The time to act is now. If Christians don't act now and wait for someday, then someday in the not too distant future there will be no conservative candidates for whom to vote. If voters fail to act, the political climate will become even more toxic. Radical ideology will become firmly embedded in the fabric of our society, and conservatism will die. Radicalism will rule the day, and the United States of America will never be great again!

C H A P T E R   5

Ravaged by Radical Politics

My people are destroyed for lack of knowledge.
Because you have rejected knowledge...
HOSEA 4:6 NKJV

Without a concerted effort on the part of the GOP to recruit true conservative candidates and a commitment of voters to elect them, the country remains on a precarious course. Currently, most major cities in the United States are being ravaged by far-left progressive politics. Mayors of these cities should make significant course corrections or be voted out of office and replaced by conservative leadership. U.S. cities run by radical Democrats are embattled with moral corruption, face financial instability and uncertainty, and are overwhelmed with lawlessness. These formerly thriving cities are now drug-infested and besieged by crime. The Bible provides a fairly accurate description of the situation in Isaiah 1:21, which reads, "How the faithful city has become a harlot! It was full of justice; righteousness lodged in it, but now murderers."

Major cities such as San Francisco, Los Angeles, St. Louis, and Washington, D.C., are not only crime-ridden but have also become hovels of demoralizing tent cities. And cities such as Baltimore, Detroit, and Chicago not only have large homeless populations, but their violence and murder rates make them appear more like war zones than cities located in the United States. Several major cities that once were safe havens *from* crime now have become safe havens *for* crime. The criminal element, in concert with radically liberal politicians, has taken over former conservative strongholds, making them sanctuaries for criminal activity.

How does a conservative stronghold become a bastion of liberalism? There's only one way: Christians have rejected the Lord's knowledge and are voting for liberal candidates who are navigating their cities to the brink of destruction. Christians need to vote righteously and reclaim spiritually shipwrecked cities for Christ. We often hear Christians who don't vote or those who vote for radicals bewailing the demise of our country and its crumbling Christian foundation, not realizing by their action or inaction that they helped create the problems for which they're now expressing regret. Many continue to vote for liberal Democrats election cycle after election cycle, foolishly anticipating a different result, while others don't bother to vote at all. Then Christians wonder why things are falling apart. It's absolutely dumbfounding and almost inconceivable that many believers support liberal politicians in open rebellion against God. The Bible says in Isaiah 1:2–3, "Hear, O heavens, and give ear, O earth! For the LORD has spoken: 'I have nourished and brought up children, and they have rebelled against Me; the ox knows its owner and the donkey its master's crib; but Israel does not know, My people do not consider [understand].'" These words were spoken to rebellious Israelites, but they could just as well have been spoken to rebellious Americans today.

Professing Christians don't have to necessarily vote for only Christian politicians, but they should vote for conservative leaders who support Christian values. Since Christians are such a large and powerful voting bloc, they're largely responsible for who's elected to political office and who's not. The loyalty of many Christians is misdirected; they continue to remain loyal to a destructive political party that long ago left them behind, if indeed it was ever with them in the first place. The party they still desperately cling to no longer represents their social mores and beliefs; it's arguable that it never did.

Based on the Democrat Party's history, it is debatable the party ever supported Christian values or ever truly represented the common man—as is often claimed. For literally decades, the Democrat Party's benevolent assertions seemingly have been falsely misrepresented and grossly exaggerated. For example, when Republicans fought to abolish slavery, Democrats fought to keep and expand it. When Republicans fought for civil rights, Democrats fought to oppose them. The Thirteenth, Fourteenth, and Fifteenth U.S. Constitutional Amendments were passed almost exclusively by Republicans. Democrats resisted and opposed equal rights for blacks for more than a century. The Thirteenth Amendment received 100 percent Republican support and less than 25 percent support from Democrats to end slavery. The Fourteenth Amendment was passed exclusively by Republicans to grant citizenship and equal rights to blacks. No Democrats voted for the Fourteenth Amendment. The Fifteenth Amendment gave voting rights to blacks; again, Republicans voted for it, and the Democrats voted against it. With a record like this, it makes one wonder why any black American would support the Democrat Party. But with a record like this, it's easy to see why the adversary could gain such a foothold in the Democrat Party.

Like many American cities, the Democrat Party is in peril and has become besieged by lawlessness. But Democrats seem to have convenient amnesia when it comes to their notorious past and inhumane treatment of minorities. Any mention of their reprehensible history is always noticeably absent. Even today, when conservatives propose meaningful legislation that benefits the country, it's vigorously resisted by Democrats. According to them, conservative Republicans are bad guys who should never be trusted! But, in reality, it's far-left Democrats who actively oppose laws benefiting ordinary Americans, and they're often responsible for introducing unsound legislation that harms the livelihood of minorities, the poor, and the middle class—and, in spite of their claims—benefits wealthy elites.

Their progressive policies tend to make things considerably worse for most citizens, while their fake compassion for naïve people—especially starry-eyed illegals—is used to garner votes that keep them in office. We can be relatively certain that in close elections, Democrats often win because of illegal votes. In fact, if illegal votes were discounted in the 2016 election, my guess is that Hillary Clinton not only didn't win the Electoral College, but she didn't win the popular vote either! Dead people get resurrected every election cycle to vote in the general election along with their cats, dogs, pet cobras, Mickey and Minnie Mouse, and a whole host of other fictional and cartoon characters. In addition to dead people, pets, and fictional characters casting votes for Democrat candidates, many illegal immigrants are also encouraged to vote for their favorite radical politicians.

While I was living in Virginia and discussing politics with my lawn-service provider in the summer of 2015, he told me that he always voted Democrat. But in November 2016, when I asked him if he had voted, he confessed that he was in the country illegally and would not be voting in the general election. I was absolutely flabbergasted, since he had told me the previous year that he was a staunch Democrat and always voted Democrat no matter what! I had no idea he was an illegal immigrant, nor that he was possibly voting illegally in our elections. But one thing I can certainly vouch for is that he had all the markings of a far-left Democrat! Although he charged the going rate for mowing our lawn, he often tried to price-gouge us for additional lawn services. At those times, my husband negotiated the price down to the reasonable, prevailing rate. In reality, this illegal immigrant was pocketing a larger profit than his legal U.S. counterparts, because as an illegal he wasn't paying taxes on his income. This man didn't attempt to overcharge us because he didn't like us as clients; just the opposite—he did it to try to take advantage of our financial success and generosity. Several times a year I gave him lavish tips so he could have lunch at our expense, and I also gave him and his illegal assistant generous Christmas bonuses. To a Republican mindset, one might expect a gracious attitude or even an occasional price break instead of an attempted price gouge. But not so with an ungrateful radical-left Democrat! With their mindset, one sees an opportunity not to reward, but to exploit the kindness and generosity of others. This is just one of the major differences between conservative

Republican and radical Democrat ethics and worldviews. With many Democrats, the attitude is *gimme, gimme, gimme, my name is Gimme, and I'll take everything that you'll give me!* Proverbs 30:15a is relevant still and accurately describes many of the new loyalists to the Democrat Party. This proverb states, "The leech has two daughters—Give and Give!"

Many illegals have an employed family member who earns a livable wage, while the spouse collects welfare or food stamps from our government. According to the Democrat Party, illegals have a right to collect financial benefits provided at the expense of American taxpayers—and anyone who disagrees is a racist. There are even rumblings of providing reparations to illegals! Radical policies such as these tend to harm poor and middle-class Americans, while rich elitists somehow manage to escape.

Some people, primarily liberals and leftists, argue that our economy would collapse without illegal immigration. They try to persuade everyone that illegals do jobs that American citizens won't do. In other words, illegals are good for us, and we owe them a debt of gratitude. That is just another big progressive lie. A lot of citizens lose their jobs when business owners decide to fire them to replace them with illegal immigrants. But if people are astute, they'll notice these businesses never lower the prices of their goods or services. This is why my husband and I boycott "*fire and replace*" businesses. Consumers realize that there are no recognizable benefits from the "*fire citizen and hire foreigner*" practices, as there is no reduction in prices and no noticeable increase in quality. In many cases, there may even be a perceptible decrease in quality. In some areas of the United States, it feels as if one is in a foreign country nowadays when trying to communicate with customer service employees. After multiple failed attempts to make oneself understood, it's best to just politely walk away and purchase the item elsewhere.

We do *not* need illegal immigration in order to survive as a country. Illegal immigration is a detriment to the United States, or any country for that matter, and we simply cannot allow it to continue. From security, safety, and economic standpoints, illegal immigration is a very bad idea, but progressives try to convince us that illegals are good for us and our economy. Liberals profess to embrace illegals wholeheartedly—but just not in their neck of the woods. While residing in Virginia, I was surprised by the disrespectful attitude and barrage of insults directed by some liberals toward illegal immigrants—behind their backs, of course. Publicly they displayed approval of minorities entering our country illegally by supporting the policies of the Obama administration, but privately they told a different story. They claimed to welcome illegal immigration, just not in their affluent neighborhoods; this is the height of hypocrisy.

Hypocrisy is also vividly demonstrated by liberal governors who insist on open borders but refuse to accept illegals from the federal government. When President Trump proposed sending illegal immigrants to sanctuary cities—surprise—Democrat politicians said *no way.* Currently, cities run by Democrats are overwhelmed with illegal aliens and approaching the breaking point. In San Francisco, Los Angeles, and several other sanctuary cities, illegals live on the streets in tents or rudely constructed shacks and use the sidewalks as outdoor restrooms, actually urinating and defecating on sidewalks and surrounding areas. The filth and stench is shocking. But this is okay with radical city leaders, state representatives, and federal politicians, as long as the illegals don't move into *their* exclusive gated communities. It's okay in our neighborhoods, just not near their ivory-tower palaces. This is hypocrisy on steroids! The love and compassion of liberal Democrats for illegals and for other poor minorities goes only as far as the neighborhoods of ordinary citizens. Their love and compassion doesn't extend to the portion of the city where they reside.

President Obama clandestinely shipped hundreds of illegals to conservative cities and states without any forewarning or prior approval. But according to liberals, President Trump doesn't have the authority to transfer illegals to areas of the country controlled by Democrats. President Trump not only has the authority to ship illegals to sanctuary cities, but he should require these cities to accept them, particularly in Democrat strongholds. They have been protecting illegals for years, while jeopardizing the lives of

U.S. citizens. Even Iranian terrorists were allowed in our country illegally in 2011, but this doesn't alarm far-left radicals. They've put out a warm *welcome mat* for all illegals in our communities, including terrorists.

Liberals now scream loudly about separating illegal parents and their children—and housing them in cages—but this policy was used extensively under the Obama administration. The cages they refer to are not actual cages, but wire enclosures. These liberals are either liars or have very, very short memories; I'm going with liars! Instead of protesting the *mistreatment* of illegals, why don't these compassionate liberals employ, house, educate, and feed all illegal immigrants residing in their cities? This would remove them from the streets and keep them from defecating in the public squares—and it might even prevent another Boston marathon–type bombing. It also would adequately fulfill the liberal social-justice agenda and prevent the social services of our government from being overwhelmed. Further, it would put the love and compassion of liberals on full display for the whole world to see, but I'm not holding my breath!

Liberals put on a good show but rarely deliver anything of value. Politicians are elected to represent our interests, but most of them have forgotten those whom they were elected to serve. They have become enamored with power and prestige, and they have set themselves up as mini-gods dictating from their imagined thrones. Their mini-god status is never more on display than when conservatives are subjected to congressional hearings on Capitol Hill. Arrogant committee members use shameful tactics to question people, showing blatant hostility and disrespect toward conservatives who are required to appear before their thrones. It's truly an appalling, shameless display of their abuse of power. The only thing that's missing is an arena where they can throw their tormented subjects to the lions! Oh, wait a minute, these politicians *are* the lions!

How obnoxious politicians, displaying such repugnant and nauseating practices on Capitol Hill, manage to stay in power is a puzzling mystery. Their maltreatment of innocent American citizens is beyond shocking. The only logical explanation for voters accepting such abusive tactics is pervasive deception and ungodliness on a massive scale. By allowing toxic politicians such as these to remain in power, their radical agenda has set a course for decimating our Constitution, completely eliminating civility, and erasing our Christian heritage.

Unfortunately, beguiled Christians are serving two masters by consenting to ungodly politics. Jesus tells us that serving two masters cannot be done successfully, nor can it be done without fatally wounding our country and jeopardizing our Christian heritage. Radical progressives have been allowed to steer the nation into hazardous waters. People must stop electing radicals to public office and abandon their sinking progressive ship.

President Trump and his administration will be able to only delay, but not stop, the inevitable from happening unless more conservatives and Christians unite as a powerful voting bloc and remove radical extremists from political office at all levels of government. Otherwise, the destruction perpetrated upon our country by extremists will eventually become permanent and inescapable. If we unite, we can win the battle against their radical ideology! It's time to get off of the *Titanic*, board a lifeboat, and head for safe ground. Trump is the lifeboat, sent from God, to help rescue us from radical-left politics and lead us to a secure and anchored political harbor!

CHAPTER 6

A Kingdom Divided

Jesus knew their thoughts, and said unto them,
"Every kingdom divided against itself is
brought to desolation; and every city or
house divided against itself shall not stand."
MATTHEW 12:25 KJV

Our country is so divided spiritually, culturally, and politically that it appears more like the Divided States of America than the United States of America. The division isn't a recent phenomenon, but partisan politics and the great divide seem to have grown considerably worse over the past several decades. Of course, we were greatly divided during the Civil War. But several decades later, a healing of sorts seemed to take place, and the political parties were at least civil to one another. Now partisan politics operates at such a level of heated hostility that civility has been almost completely lost. Many of those in Congress and elsewhere act like savage beasts with barbaric instincts, ripping and tearing each other apart. Individuals are particularly hostile to people with opposing conservative views. If radicals remain on this course, our country will implode from within. It's only by the grace of almighty God that the United States is still standing. Most nations or dynasties with this kind of internal strife and ungodliness don't last for more than a couple of centuries.

The adversary promotes radically diverse ideologies and anarchy to bring about as much strife and division as possible. His ultimate goal is to divide and conquer us as a people and a nation because he knows a divided people, house, or nation will eventually be brought to desolation.

To win the ideological war being waged within our borders, conservatives must unite and engage the battle together. Unfortunately, some conservatives, including Christians, have succumbed to lies of the enemy and are actively opposing the Kingdom of God. Some believers are serving two masters in kingdoms that are in direct opposition to one another. The Lord tells us in Matthew 6:24 that it's impossible to serve two masters, because people will love the one and hate the other, or will be loyal to one master and despise the other one. Christians trying to be loyal to two kingdoms and serving two masters are operating from a confused perspective—and unknowingly have become emissaries of the devil. Their loyalties are divided between the Kingdom of Light and the Kingdom of Darkness. They desperately try to remain committed to Christ and their Christian values and at the same time to radical-left politics. This simply cannot be done.

The adversary skillfully divides the kingdom by motivating some Christians to accept liberalism and pledge allegiance to ungodly politics. Another preferred tactic the enemy uses to deceive Christians and bring division is to make them feel, in good conscience, that they cannot support certain candidates. Some people are convinced they can only support or vote for *nearly perfect* politicians—so with a great sanctimonious attitude—they sometimes decide to sit out important elections. This generally assures a win for liberal or radical politicians, but this somehow doesn't seem to bother their conscience.

Democrats, unlike self-righteous Republicans, usually stick to their candidates like glue, never sitting out a single election to appease their conscience. This is the one thing that I almost admire about Democrats—how loyal they remain to each other during general elections! They will go to almost any length to ensure their candidate wins—lie, cheat, steal, whatever it takes to be victors.

But some Republicans, especially establishment politicians, often show disloyalty to the extreme and display a self-righteous attitude toward each other. Some of them even foolishly kill and eat their own, particularly during presidential campaigns.

Every election cycle, some of the self-righteous Republican crowd yell and screech loudly that they won't endorse or vote for the imperfect presidential nominee—he has a zit, a horrible zit, a shameful blemish on his nose! They scream with robust energy and engage the liberal mainstream media and radical Democrat politicians to help bloody and bludgeon the Republican candidate nearly to death! The self-righteous Pharisees shriek the loudest and recruit others to help them protest, while continuing to pummel the nominee with humiliating insults. Fake news media provocateurs exuberantly thrash the Republican candidate, using incendiary language to incite violence toward the loyal supporters of the tortured nominee.

The above scenario fairly accurately describes the challenges some Republican candidates, especially presidential ones, face when running for public office. Self-righteous pharisaical folks feel it's their duty to discredit certain Republican politicians and, if possible, destroy their reputations and ruin their chances of being elected. Liberals in the news media are absolutely thrilled to do their part in maiming these poor, beleaguered politicians.

Democrat Party candidates, on the other hand, are always lauded with praise for all of their wonderful attributes—even if they're acknowledged human traffickers with fifteen sex slaves living in their basement! The battle leading up to the eventual party nomination may be vicious, but once the nominee has been determined—it's all hands on deck! Democrat voters, including the liberal mainstream media and delusional Christians, promote their candidate as a highly principled person who truly loves women and is a great champion of women's rights; a wonderful family guy or gal; a pillar of society; a patriot and stellar citizen of the community with impeccable character and divine motives; and a lover of the *little guy*—even the fifteen sex slaves chained in the basement! (This describes the loyalty of Democrats, with only slight exaggeration.) On the other hand, invariably, self-righteous

Republicans oppose their candidate and savagely impugn the candidate's character. The Republican nominee's unsightly zit poses more of a problem for some conservatives than the probable election of a radical left-wing psychopath. They unreasonably strain at a tiny gnat, while swallowing a whole camel.

Yep, the enemy has executed his work well and divided the kingdom by using individuals with sanctimonious attitudes to oppose candidates, while feeling extremely self-righteous and good about themselves. As I stated previously, the other method the adversary uses to divide the kingdom is convincing some conservatives to accept radical ideology and support ungodly politicians. Even the Lord Himself must feel exasperated at times by the large number of people who fall for these tactics.

The thinking of deceived individuals has become marred by liberal rhetoric, and they've been persuaded to despise President Trump—making them unable to view him realistically. Some accuse him of divisiveness and racism, claiming they've heard him openly admit to abhorring everyone but white people. Incredibly, these individuals actually *do hear* President Trump say *things he hasn't said,* because their deceitful hearts lie to them and blind their reality. The Bible tells us in 1 John 2:11, "He who hates his brother is in darkness and walks in darkness, and does not know where he is going, because the darkness has blinded his eyes."

How can reasonably intelligent people fall for such obvious lies? And how does anyone fall for the big lie—that Democrats are good, and Republicans are evil? After being treated with disrespect and booted from the debate stage, one of the 2020 Democrat presidential hopefuls suddenly realized that Democrats are nasty people. She indicated that she had always thought Democrats were good guys, and Republicans were the bad guys. I like this particular candidate, even though my worldview, theology, and political ideology are the complete opposite of hers. Although I would never vote for her, I would love to meet her and introduce her to Jesus. When I read her biography on Wikipedia, I could relate to her and identify with much of her life story—especially in her early twenties. She was messed up, living an immoral lifestyle, searching for answers, and looking for love in all the wrong places! After reading her biography, I recognized she is what could best be described as one of those *old-time liberals,* one who actually has compassion for others and truly wants to help the less fortunate. While her political doctrine mirrors that of the Democrat Party, her compassion for others doesn't fit with that of most Democrat politicians. I'm not saying all Democrats are bad guys, and all Republicans are good guys. This clearly is not the case, but the ideology of the Republican Party more closely aligns with a biblical worldview, while that of the Democrats is solidly unbiblical.

The majority of people belonging to the Republican Party, including President Trump, promote biblical values of love and inclusion. To say that Trump encourages division and despises minorities is just another big manufactured lie of the radical left. President Trump is a friend of minorities, and he encourages unity and peace among the races; the same cannot honestly be said about many Democrats. While some see Trump as an enemy of minorities, others praise him for his pro-minority stance. Much of the legislation he has signed places him firmly in the category of friend. His policies have provided incentives for investing in minority communities and other distressed areas of the country, resulting in increased economic opportunities for blacks and other minorities. President Trump's policies also have promoted minority-owned business opportunities and provided additional funding for historically black colleges and universities. Additionally, legislation to reform the criminal justice system—called the First Step Act—impacts minorities in a positive way by reducing prison sentences for certain crimes, promoting early release, creating more effective rehabilitation programs that help reduce recidivism rates, and providing better training for inmates to assist them in reentering the workforce so they can become productive members of society. The First Step Act has been welcomed by minorities who experience disproportionally higher incarceration rates. Some minorities were eligible for immediate release upon the signing of this important piece of legislation into law. (This is a great piece of legislation with one caveat—that only non-violent criminals be granted early release from prison; otherwise, this law potentially could backfire very badly.)

Radical politicians and the liberal media have eviscerated the truth about President Trump, and they also refuse to give the president any credit for the extraordinary things he and his administration have accomplished. Radical Democrats are still desperately trying to impose crimes on the president that they themselves are guilty of, and they have ludicrously voted to impeach him—not because of his guilt, but because of his innocence!

Radicals accuse the president of quid pro quo, bribery, obstruction of justice, collusion, inciting violence, and the list goes on. They're guilty of all of these things and more. After their outrageous rhetoric sparks ruthless behavior in others, it suddenly becomes the fault of President Trump and his conservative supporters. All of this makes one wonder about their mental stability and calls into question whether *any* Democrat politician has the mental capacity or temperament to serve at any level of our government. We always experience setbacks in race relations, our justice system, and in religious liberty under their radical leadership. Unlike adversarial actions of radicals, President Trump's leadership has been good for us and our country.

If history were to evaluate Trump's presidency fairly and without liberal bias, from God's perspective, he would surely be acclaimed as one of the greatest U.S. presidents ever! It's doubtful, however, that enough impartial political scientists and godly historians exist in our country to rank the presidency of Trump fairly and honestly. There probably isn't enough godliness or intellectual integrity among the group of "experts" to properly assess the value of any of our presidents. For them to evaluate leaders properly, they need to assess them using God's wisdom and see leaders from God's viewpoint instead of assessing them from their own flawed ideological worldview. The presidential rankings of Trump and Obama will indicate whether historians are evaluating them from a Kingdom of Light or Kingdom of Darkness perspective. The Bible says in Isaiah 5:20, "Woe to those who call evil good, and good evil; who substitute darkness for light and light for darkness; who substitute bitter for sweet and sweet for bitter!" (NASB).

Only history will reveal from which kingdom perspective political science scholars will view Trump's presidency and that of Obama and other recent presidents. If they are liberals, or are influenced by pharisaical Republicans and radical Democrats, their evaluation of President Trump isn't likely to be very honest or favorable. But if they assess Trump's presidency with intellectual honesty based strictly on his many admirable accomplishments, disregarding all the defamatory rhetoric, then he likely would achieve the second position in the rankings—with perhaps President Abraham Lincoln still holding on to the number-one spot. For President Trump to get a fair shake now or in the future, historians must ignore the acrimonious comments made by dishonest politicians, unethical journalists, and other devious individuals opposing him.

Abraham Lincoln is considered by most people to be our greatest president ever, but this certainly wasn't always the case. Our country then, as it is now, was so divided politically that Honest Abe was the country's most hated and vilified man. But history has now rewritten a vastly different narrative of this great man's life. Perhaps President Trump's story will someday be presented honestly—maybe not; the chasm may now be too wide to span. Our country has become so badly divided by partisan politics that it may never be truly united again.

The enemy stirs up strife and orchestrates division among politicians and other citizens because he knows a country or government divided against itself cannot stand forever. As indicated in John 10:10, the adversary's ultimate goal is to kill, steal, and destroy. The ungodly recklessness of radicals can only be demonically choreographed. Case in point, why would educated people support socialism or communism in America when any sensible person knows what has happened historically in every socialist and communist country throughout the world? Yet, the adversary promotes preposterous ideals through radical ideology designed to decimate the United States. He convinces unwary individuals that socialism would be good for us.

The enemy's goal is to divide us and defeat conservatism by instilling far-left progressive ideology into the hearts and minds of gullible people. The devil knows that if he can promote radicalism and precipitate long-term division, then the battle will be won. Our adversary is working toward the fulfillment of Matthew 12:25 by fostering strife, anarchy, and incivility. He is continuously working toward his destructive goal of division by pitting politician against politician, liberal against conservative, race against race, gender against gender, and even Christian against Christian. The divisiveness is clearly working, causing people to be uncivil and sometimes even barbaric toward each other. In the meantime, the devil and his forces are having a very good day!

Without a significant change in people's attitudes, the great divide imposed by the adversary will become too vast to span. Our sharply divided Congress is particularly troubling. Many congressional members are filled with so much malice it seems unlikely they can accomplish the job they were elected to do. Virtually all of their time is spent attacking biblical values and angrily opposing the president's conservative agenda; no time is left for governing.

One bitter Congresswoman is so unhinged that she believes she's on a mission from God to destroy President Trump. She clearly is on a mission from the evil one and someday will stand before the Lord and give account for her actions. If she doesn't repent and change her behavior, she should not be surprised to hear the Lord Jesus Christ speak these words to her from Matthew 7:23, "I never knew you; depart from Me, you who practice lawlessness!" One can only imagine what the Jewish Jesus will say to other radicals in Congress, the media, academia, and the entertainment or business world who are of Jewish ancestry—all wasted intelligence and squandered lives.

The only way to salvage our country and recover from a gravely divided Congress is to vote all radicals out of office, including liberal Republicans masquerading as conservatives. There will never be peace or agreement between radicals and conservatives because their worldviews are polar opposites and incompatible with each other. This is why a Congress divided between radicals and conservatives cannot work successfully. They have irreconcilable differences and no common ground from which to work or negotiate. The only solution is to replace liberal and radical politicians at all levels of our government.

We must choose national leaders who are wise enough not to involve us in unnecessary wars, who won't depose foreign leaders needlessly, and who won't interfere with foreign elections. In the past, we've elected presidents who've started wars they wouldn't finish and caused chaos by unnecessarily deposing foreign governmental officials and meddling in some foreign government elections. Unless foreign governments represent a legitimate threat to our national security, our country shouldn't interfere with them. It would be wise for us to take care of problems at home and leave the running of other countries to their leaders. Ousting nonthreatening foreign rulers or interfering in foreign elections is not our business. We need to take care of our own home and leave the care of our neighbor's home to them. Let President Putin run Russia, Prime Minister Netanyahu govern Israel, and other leaders run their respective countries. Until we repair our own house and mend our own fences, we shouldn't be trying to fix our neighbor's. We should be working to make more allies, not fewer, and to win more friends, not make more enemies.

Governing the United States of America is a daunting task. Successfully running any country—whether ruled by elected officials or a reigning monarch—takes enormous effort, so we would be wise to concentrate on governing our own country and allowing other countries to govern themselves. We shouldn't interfere with other countries, unless they present a serious threat to the United States or our allies. Voters would be wise to take this into consideration when choosing our leaders and vote for presidents who will deal appropriately with foreign rulers.

The political climate has grown so toxic in America and in much of the rest of the world that voters would be wise to use more godly wisdom when selecting national leaders, not less—and elect more principled leaders, not less ethical ones.

CHAPTER 7

Could Jesus Get Elected in the United States?

Do not imitate what is evil, but what is good.
He who does good is of God,
but he who does evil has not seen God.

3 JOHN 11 NKJV

In our current political climate, it's questionable and perhaps highly unlikely that Jesus Christ could get elected today in the United States of America. Modern-day Pharisees, the "*holier-than-thou*" club, along with their friends on the left would work together feverishly to try and ensure the defeat of the candidacy of Jesus. These two elitist groups, who often are at odds with each other, are in reality essentially the flipside of the same coin. They're both radical, both are wrong, and both groups are bent on destroying our country one way or another while claiming to be patriots. The radicals and the Pharisees despise and threaten anyone who doesn't agree completely with their philosophy and self-righteous viewpoint. They intimidate and harass people and try to compel them to accept their perspective. Far-left radicals, along with some elitist Pharisees, have all but taken over the mainstream media, academia, social media, the entertainment industry, and local, state, and federal governments. They use the mainstream media to give voice to and promote their self-serving agendas. Both the Republican Pharisees and the radical Democrats, many of whom are journalists, use the media to convince naïve people that what they read in print, hear on television, or see on social media should be trusted unequivocally and isn't to be questioned by anyone. Radicals and Pharisees in the media have enlisted the aid of Hollywood and college campuses to spread their diabolical ideology. These two groups, who don't represent the values of conservative Americans, unfortunately have also managed to infiltrate our local, state, and federal governments. They have long been a menace to the health and security of our country. Some establishment Republicans have also been known to joyfully join the ranks of the radical left and the Pharisees to undermine conservative Republicans. Their irresponsible actions ravage the country, are careless of our values, and negatively impact virtually every area of our lives.

Far-left progressives and liberal elites, who normally mock Pharisees and establishment Republicans and try to maim them, gladly accept their perspective when their opinions can be used to injure conservatives. The liberal media is especially adept at destroying the reputations of conservative political candidates, and they always gleefully welcome any negative input from self-righteous Pharisees. In fact, often the information provided by Pharisees is harsher and more damaging to conservatives than that of their liberal counterparts. Their self-righteous furor can be absolutely brutal, unbelievably ruthless, and even savage when attacking those conservatives with whom they disagree. This being said, now let's develop a scenario in which the Lord Jesus Christ shows up in our country and announces His candidacy for president of the United States.

Liberal journalists would jump on this story right away, each one trying to outdo the other and be first to report the unexpected news. Liberal television network executives and leftist newspapers across the land would quickly concoct stories to destroy the reputation of Jesus and sabotage His campaign. Every outlet would fervently attack Jesus with a vengeance like never seen before—much harsher treatment than that inflicted upon Lincoln and Trump combined.

The *Washington Post* headline might scream, with story following:

Fanatical Rabbi Jesus Announces Candidacy!

The most radical and conservative candidate ever to hit the political scene is a candidate by the name of Rabbi Jesus Christ. His claims and political platform are so outlandish that it's almost impossible to take him seriously. But for some unknown reason, immediately after announcing his bid for president, his poll numbers have shot through the roof! Actually, he began gaining approval among evangelical and charismatic Christians while he was still toying with the idea of running. But now he has made it official and has jumped into the race. But folks, we must warn you, his ideas are outrageous, and his tweets are borderline insane. Rabbi Jesus has even asserted on more than one occasion that he is God and that he has supernatural powers to heal people. It makes one wonder how the Rabbi can make such bizarre statements, and yet still be popular with potential voters. It's mysterious and extremely alarming, to say the least. Actually, it's downright unsettling. It's also rather baffling that Rabbi Jesus is apparently running virtually unopposed on the Republican Party ticket. In fact, he is already considered by some to be the presumptive nominee.

The favored Democrat candidate (Lady Socialist) faces a slight battle, challenging 36 other opponents for the nomination of her party. But most of her challengers concede that she will most likely be the Democrat Party nominee. Many progressives, especially millennials, see the other candidates as too old, too tired, too white, too Jewish, too boring, or too much a part of the establishment to be viable candidates. Lady Socialist, on the other hand, is young and energetic, with respectable poll numbers. And her poll numbers are expected to rise sharply after she secures the nomination. But her campaign could potentially be in trouble, unless the Rabbi can be stopped! Perhaps this initial furor over Rabbi Jesus will simply dissipate and blow over in the weeks to come. But, sadly, based on what has taken place in recent elections, we cannot take anything for granted. We must not make the same mistake again by being overly confident in this election. Unless Rabbi Jesus is stopped quickly before his campaign gains more momentum, we fear he may push our esteemed candidate's campaign over a cliff—even before it gets off the ground. There is one encouraging thread of light streaming through all of this, though: Some of the establishment Republicans and many far-right Pharisees don't approve of the Rabbi and have emphatically stated they will not be endorsing his candidacy. Many distinguished colleagues from the Rabbi's own party have made several disparaging comments about the candidate; surely they have valid reasons for not endorsing him. We will speak to them in more depth and get back to our valued readers on this issue. Stay tuned. Things are bound to get interesting!

This will be an election like no other in the history of our country, but we must caution voters early in this election cycle not to be misled by the hype and unfounded claims of Rabbi Jesus. Clearly, he does not represent the mores and values of our country. The Rabbi appears to be delusional at times and seems to suffer from schizophrenia; it's been reported that he has dual personalities. It is our duty as patriotic Americans, for the survival of our country and all that we hold dear, to consider seriously this election and decide whether we can trust a man like the Rabbi in our nation's capital. All patriotic Americans must ask themselves: Can a religious, schizophrenic fanatic like Rabbi Jesus be trusted with our future and the future of our children?

Immediately following the publication of the *Washington Post* article and similar articles in newspapers all across the land, the DNC and other progressives leap into action and begin strategizing how best to destroy the Rabbi's reputation and torpedo His campaign. The first order of business for the "Defeat Jesus" team is to identify individuals and groups of individuals who can be trusted to support the cause—defeating Rabbi Jesus and ensuring Lady Socialist is crowned the next president of the United States. They take an inventory of those already in the tank with them—journalists from CNN, MSNBC, and all mainstream media television networks, social media moguls, CEOs of leftist newspapers and magazines and their journalism staffs, progressives from labor and commercial businesses, late-night television hosts, liberal Hollywood directors, writers, producers, actors and actresses, progressive authors and political activists, liberal sports figures, current and former elitist politicians, pastors of liberal and social-justice churches, indoctrinated millennials, radicalized schoolteachers and college professors, and unelected employees of the Deep State. The progressives realize they have acquired quite a following over the years, an impressive group indeed, but they cannot afford to leave anything to chance. The Rabbi must be defeated! They've learned that the Pharisees despise the Rabbi, so perhaps this can be used to their advantage to help them prevent Rabbi Jesus from being elected. Since the progressive group might not be large enough or clever enough to defeat Rabbi Jesus on their own, members of the group decide it would be wise to recruit their most-trusted friends from among the Pharisees and "Never Trumpers," including Little Billy War Hawk, Baseball George Pulitzer, a few folks from Fox News, and perhaps Long Face Annie Smart Mouth. Smart Mouth has been known to call Trump an idiot on occasion, but can she be trusted to remain loyal to the cause? The progressives know Smart Mouth has been critical of the Rabbi in the past, accusing Him of being far too meek, overly trusting, unreasonably mild-mannered, and much too doggone forgiving. But they've also heard that Annie is a follower of Rabbi Jesus on Twitter, and she might actually support His candidacy. Horror of horrors if that proved to be true, and they allowed her in their group of trusted allies. They decide it might not be prudent to invite Annie to join the "Defeat Jesus" team. On the other hand, they are confident they can trust the other Pharisees and "Never Trumpers," who seem to have an almost unreasonable, deep-seated hatred for the Rabbi.

Once the group is finally assembled, a meeting is convened to discuss the best strategy for defeating the Rabbi. The team must act quickly to stop Rabbi Jesus, or at least slow down His momentum to allow time for Lady Socialist, working with the DNC, to eliminate her competition and to mount her crusade against the Rabbi. The progressives, "Never Trumpers," and Pharisees discuss a number of possible avenues and smear campaigns to tarnish the Rabbi's appeal to the ignorant masses. Since Rabbi Jesus is running essentially unopposed against their beloved Democrat candidate, Lady Socialist, they must devise a clever plan to confuse and divide the loyalties of Republican voters, then win Independent voters to their side. The idea of possibly paying a handsome, popular celebrity to run as a third-party candidate to steal votes from the Rabbi is discussed but then quickly abandoned. The progressives, "Never Trumpers," and Pharisees delve into the history of Rabbi Jesus to hatch a diabolical plan to perplex voters and make them question the Rabbi's suitability for office. Their plan must be designed to present Rabbi Jesus in the most negative light possible, and devious enough to make Republican voters stay home and cause Independent voters to turn out on Election Day for Lady Socialist. The progressives hope to win over some of the Rabbi's most faithful and ardent supporters, which would send a clear message to other conservatives, making them question their perception of Rabbi Jesus.

A number of angles are discussed by the "Defeat Jesus" team on how to paint an unbecoming and even sinister portrait of the Rabbi. The team starts by looking into the Rabbi's background and comparing it to His current political platform. The progressives, with the Pharisees' valuable input, learn that Rabbi Jesus was raised in an Orthodox Jewish home by fanatically religious parents. They also discover the Rabbi has lived most of His adult life abroad in Israel, which brought up a question about His citizenship. But when this issue was raised by several news outlets, the Rabbi's campaign manager assured journalists that Jesus was indeed a citizen of the United States and held dual/multiple citizenships around the world. The group discusses whether to investigate the Rabbi's citizenship further and ask Him to produce a valid birth certificate. But they decide this would make them appear like petty copycats if they pursued this angle since the same topic had come up in a previous presidential election. So, they decide to drop the citizenship issue altogether.

Next the group discusses the marital status of Rabbi Jesus, and congratulates all the faithful commentators and journalists on the team who've already stormed the battlefield against the enemy. A CNN commentator reports that even though Rabbi Jesus has never been married, according to His campaign manager He is an often-sought-after bachelor. They all laugh and say in unison, "Sought by whom?" Then Angry Joe shares a story relating to an interview with the Rabbi on MSNBC. When a MSNBC commentator asked Rabbi Jesus why He had never married, the Rabbi said He was still praying for His bride. The Rabbi also indicated that He initially had hoped to marry a Jewish wife but had later expanded His search to include Gentiles. The MSNBC commentator was clearly taken aback by this strange pronouncement, so the Rabbi was then asked to explain exactly what He meant by "Gentiles." Rabbi Jesus accommodated the request by explaining that Gentiles included any ethnic group other than Jews. The Rabbi then launched into a lengthy and very bizarre discussion about His perfect* future bride, and it literally made the MSNBC commentator's eyes glaze over. Fortunately, MSNBC took a commercial break so the commentator could collect herself. When she came back on the air, the commentator asked the panel of pundits if they could follow anything the Rabbi had said. The pundits went on a tirade of humiliating remarks directed toward Rabbi Jesus. (*Note: All born-again believers are called the bride of Christ.)

Another network journalist asked the Rabbi's campaign manager, "if Rabbi Jesus were elected, how would the First Lady situation be handled?" The news commentator mockingly asked Him if perhaps the perfect bride that the Rabbi had been seeking for so long would suddenly manifest and fill the role of First Lady. The campaign manager explained that Rabbi Jesus planned to adopt a surrogate to fill the role of First Lady. According to His campaign manager, the Rabbi is currently recruiting a *First Couple* to fill the role of First Lady. Evidently, the wife will be a proxy First Lady so to speak, and her husband will be a special advisor to the president. The "Defeat Jesus" team gives Angry Joe a rousing round of applause for sharing this bit of information.

The team members continue to discuss the best approach for addressing the Rabbi's single lifestyle. Then one of the Pharisees in the group asks if the team perhaps should consider either stating outright or at least insinuating that Rabbi Jesus is a homosexual. The team discusses whether or not an allegation of homosexuality would offend some of His more conservative voters and curb His appeal among Christians. This scenario is pondered at some length. It is decided that the Rabbi might lose a few far-right voters. On the other hand, this could cause Rabbi Jesus to gain more support from the LGBTQ community. Several conservative gays and lesbians are already fully committed to the Rabbi's "Make America Right Again" campaign. So, the "Defeat Jesus" team decide, by an almost unanimous vote, that it is safer to characterize Rabbi Jesus as homophobic; a homophobic rabbi was likely to anger Independent voters and scare the LGBTQs into supporting Lady Socialist. The team also decides to portray Rabbi Jesus as an egotistical prima donna who is too self-centered to have a wife and family. The team suggests a rather long list of other terms to describe the Rabbi, including *mentally incompetent, scary, evil, untrustworthy, bigoted, racist, superficial, immoral, unloving, unkind, rude, pathological liar, obnoxious*, and a whole host of other descriptive adjectives.

While looking into the Rabbi's background, the team discovers that Rabbi Jesus, as an adult, had surrounded Himself with a group of Jews—all men. Not a single female was included in His insider group. Most of the Rabbi's closest friends and associates were foul-mouthed fishermen who clung to their religious scrolls and fishing poles. Even in their religious gatherings, women were told to remain silent and be submissive to their husbands! From this bit of information, the team decides the Rabbi is clearly a sexist. He obviously doesn't like women. Not only were most of His closest friends restricted to only Jewish males, He also sometimes insulted other ethnic groups—actually calling them "dogs"! The "Defeat Jesus" team was absolutely ecstatic to find this bit of information. It was determined by the group that Rabbi Jesus is unquestionably both a sexist and a racist! The "Defeat Jesus" team members also ascertain from the Rabbi's past and current comments relating to little children that He is definitely pro-life. They are certain the Rabbi intends to abolish abortion. *Roe v. Wade* is in serious jeopardy, and women's health care is at risk. The group perceives that the Rabbi's hatred toward women is almost unfathomable, and they cannot understand His huge following among conservative women. The team is quick to label these women as sick, detestable traitors to their own gender.

The "Defeat Jesus" team also discusses how narcissistic Rabbi Jesus is. Then a long discussion ensues about the many statements and outrageous claims the Rabbi has made in the past and since announcing His candidacy. One of the Pharisees states what he thinks should be obvious to everyone—even the candidate's most radical Christian constituency: The Rabbi is clearly a fanatical religious nut job! The "Defeat Jesus" team leader, Mr. Progressive Bigshot, says, "The Rabbi is always claiming, 'I am this, I am that, I am, I am, I am!' He claims He is God and the Son of God. He claims to be a miracle worker, able to control the weather and heal the sick, and He proposes doing away with most health care programs. His policies will essentially put doctors, nurses, and a lot of health care providers out of work and destroy the profits of large pharmaceutical companies. Lobbyists in the medical industry are incensed and clamoring to defeat His campaign. People are really worried about the future of health care in our country. When the Rabbi was asked how He plans to heal everybody, He admitted that not everyone will get healed. That is why the country will still need some hospitals, pharmacies, and health care providers. Then, when the Rabbi was pressed further on this issue, He had the unmitigated nerve to tell journalists that He understands their skepticism. That might be the understatement of many centuries! According to Him, skeptics won't get healed—how convenient for Him! But He is supposedly commissioning many of His supporters to also heal people by transferring some of His supernatural powers to them. What a ploy! We must expose this man for the fraud He obviously is. I still cannot understand His appeal. I've heard that the Rabbi also often publicly tells people that He forgives their sins. They don't even have to meet Him or a priest in a confessional booth! He even insists He can raise the dead. No wonder He thinks He is God!"

Everybody on the "Defeat Jesus" team laughs hysterically. But their laughter belies their deep concern that Rabbi Jesus might actually become president of the United States, unless they can sway His supporters to abandon Him. Mr. Bigshot screams, "Rabbi Jesus is absolutely, without any doubt whatsoever, a bona-fide lunatic! He is not only a narcissist, but He is a *delusional* narcissist!" The entire team is clearly traumatized by the prospect of a fanatical rabbi becoming president of the United States, and they begin lamenting the conservative evils sure to follow if the "Defeat Jesus" team is unsuccessful.

Little Billy War Hawk is distressed that the meeting appears to be wrapping up with no mention of the issue closest to his heart, the Rabbi's foreign policy stance. He voices his concerns about Rabbi Jesus appearing too mild in His demeanor, always calling for peace and for people to love their enemies. Little Billy says, "Imagine a foreign policy posture of loving one's enemies and expecting peace, how terribly naïve of the foolish Rabbi. His lack of good judgment is essentially opening the floodgates to evil regimes and inviting our enemies to bring disaster upon us! The Rabbi apparently has no plan to confront our country's deadliest enemies. He's a peacenik, with no understanding of world affairs, who evidently plans to just love our enemies into submission. Rabbi Jesus' attitude is both foolhardy and dangerous. He is a grave danger to the security of the United States and the rest of the world. We must elect a president who fully understands this, who embraces our role in the world and our position on the international stage. The only true solution and truly successful option the United States has against our enemies is war—war, not peace, but *war*! We need to go to war with Russia; we should be at war with Iran; we need to decimate Syria; we need to decapitate North Korea. There are a number of other countries that should also be on our radar. We must cut the head off of the snake, but this silly, starry-eyed preacher wants to love our enemies to death. He's immature, He is ill-advised by the ignorant foreign policy advisors surrounding Him, and He has no idea what He is doing, but He has all of these moonstruck Christians running around fawning all over Him. If the Rabbi is elected, His policies will get us all killed! Although I'm not a fan of Lady Socialist, anybody, and I do mean *any candidate*, is better than Rabbi Jesus. Anybody but the maniac Rabbi!"

Then Baseball George speaks up to go on record as agreeing with Little Billy War Hawk. George believes the Rabbi is a menace not only to national security, but also to anyone who does not support the Rabbi's radical brand of Christianity. Baseball George sees Rabbi Jesus as a very clear and present danger to atheists and other non-Christian groups. Both Little Billy and Baseball George confess they are not exactly enamored with Lady Socialist and her radical policies, but they see Rabbi Jesus as the greater threat to democracy and world peace. Everybody nods in agreement, and all the progressives reassure Baseball George Pulitzer and Little Billy War Hawk just how happy they are that the two of them decided to join the team.

At this point, Small Man Pharisee speaks up to add credence to the comments made by both Little Billy and Baseball George. He indicates that he has done extensive research into Rabbi Jesus' past, and shares his knowledge of the Rabbi's background with the team. Small Man shares with the group how the Rabbi was once viewed as an inspiring leader who would free His adopted country from foreign oppression. But that is not what happened. Rather than defending His adopted people, the Rabbi seemed to be colluding with the foreigners. He never raised any objections or resistance against them or addressed any of the serious issues confronting His people, but only spoke love and peace, peace and love! Naturally, most of the people became disillusioned with the Rabbi's lack of leadership and rebelled against Him. Small Man has also learned from his research that Rabbi Jesus was initially very popular with the masses, was well-educated, and was sought out for His great wisdom. Small Man also confirms that the Rabbi had traveled extensively, lived abroad for many years, and had been granted citizenship in multiple countries. Small Man also imparts to the team how erratic the Rabbi's behavior seemed to be at times toward other people. Small Man tells the assembled group that Rabbi Jesus often spoke of love and peace, but His behavior frequently spoke otherwise. He evidently once went into a synagogue and beat the religious leaders with a whip. He also apparently had called some of them "snakes" and "vipers," and even "children of the devil"! The Rabbi's attitude was intolerant toward religion—except for His own brand. Further, both He and His stepfather insisted that all immigrants had to convert to their form of religion before being accepted into the country. The Rabbi obviously was opposed to any immigration, unless immigrants agreed to denounce their former cultures and adopt Christianity. Foreigners were required to totally assimilate into the Jewish communities—no exceptions. Rabbi Jesus often insulted people of other races, except the Romans, for whom He seemed to have great affection. Small Man also shares that most people who were formerly infatuated with the Rabbi soon became hostile toward Him and His method of leadership. The religious leaders were particularly offended by the Rabbi's obnoxious attitude. They distrusted Him, wanted His regime overthrown, and even wanted Him assassinated. It was purported by Rabbi Jesus and a few of His most loyal followers at the time, that the religious leaders had paid someone to have Him crucified *literally*, and later He supposedly came back to life. Small Man raises his voice loudly, almost shouting, "This is the most preposterous and outrageous claim that has been made by the Rabbi and His followers! Lady Socialist will surely slaughter Him in the general election once more people learn how appalling and hideous many of His statements and actions have been. Anyway, I just wanted to add my voice to the voices of Little Billy and Baseball George. The Rabbi is the biggest peril of our time, and He will jeopardize our very lives. He must be stopped!"

The "Defeat Jesus" team is extremely alarmed by these revelations, and they are more determined than ever to destroy the Rabbi's chances of winning the election. All of them vow not to allow this man to become president of the United States—no matter what!

The team leader then asks about the Rabbi's material wealth and how He earned that wealth. Small Man Pharisee informs the group that the Rabbi and His stepfather were formerly real estate developers. Another group member indicates that she had heard that Rabbi Jesus was merely a small-time, often unemployed carpenter. It was confirmed to the team by Small Man that the Rabbi had, indeed, been a poor carpenter early in His career. But later He and His stepfather worked tirelessly together for a number of years to build a beautiful city called Sepphoris that sat on top of a hill. This lovely city could be seen for miles around from neighboring cities because it was framed with many lights and perched high upon the mountain. Sepphoris was not only famous for its beauty and lovely architecture, but it also contained royal palaces. Evidently, Rabbi Jesus and His stepfather had a lucrative real estate development business, as they had been employed to build the city for the reigning royal family at the time. But strangely enough, neither the Rabbi nor His stepfather acquired any real material wealth from their real estate ventures. It's supposed that Rabbi Jesus and His stepfather were philanthropists who gave all their money to the poor. Small Man Pharisee tells the team that he learned after the death of the Rabbi's stepfather, Rabbi Jesus became an itinerant preacher. Mr. Bigshot chimes in, "The Rabbi has no money and has asked the GOP to fund hotly contested Senate races. His campaign evidently will be funded on hope, prayer, and pennies from little old widows." Small Man says sarcastically, "Could any of us ever have imagined a few years ago that a poor, ignorant Jewish preacher would be running for president of the United States? But I guess after Trump, anything is possible. This truly is the land of unlimited opportunity!" Mr. Bigshot then exclaims, "Funny that you mention Trump. Did you notice the strange parallels between the early lives of the Rabbi and Trump? But they pursued vastly different paths later in life, no similarities at all. That imbecile Donald Trump would never become a poor preacher or give all of his wealth away, but he's fully on board the Rabbi's 'Make American Right Again' ark. I never thought words like these would ever come out of my mouth, but we now have a buffoon even worse than Trump running for office. He must be stopped; all options are on the table. No scandal is too grandiose or scheme too ruthless; the Rabbi has to be stopped—period! One of the worst mistakes we ever made was allowing Trump to become president of the United States. Now he and his band of illiterate misfits are supporting the Rabbi's campaign." The entire team laughs heinously and applauds Mr. Bigshot for his insight.

Then some of the progressives bring up the subject of global warming. A short discussion ensues, but everybody agrees that most followers of the Rabbi aren't concerned about climate change. Besides, Rabbi Jesus claims to be able to control the weather. He supposedly commanded a storm to cease that was threatening a venue where a huge crowd was gathered to hear Him speak. Nobody could determine how He did it, but the raging storm immediately ceased. And it was reported that the Rabbi received a standing ovation that lasted over twenty minutes. At the same event, several people were supposedly healed of debilitating diseases. This story was reported both by the *Washington Journal* and FOX News on the *FOX and Friends* program. The *Journal* lauded the Rabbi for His speech and miracle-working powers, and the *F&F* crew was absolutely delirious! The entire "Defeat Jesus" team agrees that these supposed supernatural events had somehow been staged by the Rabbi's campaign staff.

Mr. Progressive Bigshot then asks some of the minority members of the group how difficult it will be to keep their black and Hispanic constituents committed to voting for Lady Socialist. He reminds them to inform the voters in their districts that Rabbi Jesus plans to do away with all government entitlements except for the infirmed. He tells them about how the Rabbi believes churches should care for orphans and widows financially; the government should support the infirmed only; and everybody else should work and pay their own way. Lady Socialist, on the other hand, plans to raise taxes on the rich and middle class to pay the way for individuals who don't particularly care to work, to sit at home and do the things they truly enjoy. Mr. Bigshot also expresses to the minority group how concerned the Democrat Party is about the "Walkaway Movement." The party is concerned about all those who have chosen to walk away and is particularly worried about the large number of minorities doing so. Mr. Bigshot warns his minority brothers and sisters on the team that without the minority vote, their beloved Democrat Party will die a quick and painful death. He asks the minority leaders to pledge their support in helping the party keep the minorities in their Democrat safety corrals. He asks the leaders to keep unrelenting pressure on their constituents not to leave the party, and to remind them that Rabbi Jesus won't continue to keep sustaining them through government programs. Mr. Progressive Bigshot stresses again the importance of minority support for the Democrat Party, because the party has no future and cannot survive without people of color and other marginalized groups. Then, Mr. Bigshot, along with several minority leaders, go on a rampage—blasting Brandon Straka—the man behind the ill-conceived Walkaway Campaign. Mr. Religious Extortionist explodes, "Who does he think he is, and who does he think he represents? He evidently thinks he is a modern-day Harriet Tubman, trying to rescue blacks and other minorities from the big, bad Democrats! Brandon is a disgrace to the LGBTQ community, and he and his little band of misfits should be ashamed of themselves. We don't need to be rescued by Brandon or anybody else. This young man needs to wake up because he's now a delirious victim who needs to be rescued himself!"

Before adjourning the meeting, Mr. Bigshot asks the team to commit to another meeting after the primary election is over to assess their success in defaming the Rabbi. He reiterates all the actions to be taken by the team. The entire team, at every opportunity, will portray Rabbi Jesus as sexist, racist, pro-life, narcissistic, homophobic, and a religious fanatic. The team of liberal journalists also plans to question the Rabbi's mental capacity, and they have a whole myriad of other lies in their hip pocket to spring on the electorate at just the right time. The team agrees that all the lies must be presented in such a way as to be believable to the average blue-collar worker and Christian enthusiast. Mr. Bigshot also informs the "Defeat Jesus" team that an emergency meeting may be called at any time, if deemed necessary.

Mr. Bigshot asks some of his most trusted allies to meet with him briefly after the meeting is adjourned to discuss another issue. He explains to the smaller group of loyalists that he is cautiously optimistic that Lady Socialist will defeat Rabbi Jesus, and he wants to ensure that all avenues are covered. He cautions this smaller group of progressives that they must have a failsafe, backup plan just in case Lady Socialist's campaign gets in trouble. Mr. Bigshot is concerned the Democrats may not be able to hold on to many of their minority voters, especially the black and Latino Christians. He expresses his anger about the Johnson Amendment being revoked because now pastors are free to endorse conservative candidates without fear of reprisal. Mr. Bigshot is also especially incensed about the Walkaway Campaign, and he expresses his fury once again toward Brandon Straka. After several more minutes of cursing and fuming directed toward President Trump and the modern-day abolitionist Harriet Tubman, Mr. Bigshot springs his biggest, boldest, and most diabolical scheme on the assembled group: If their initial efforts to defeat the Rabbi are not successful, then they'll have no other alternative but to portray Rabbi Jesus as a pedophile! Mr. Progressive Bigshot tells the group that they may even have to go so far as faking a kidnapping of two young boys, and then have them accuse the Rabbi of sexually molesting them. This would be sure to repel many of Rabbi Jesus' Christian supporters. At this, some of the "Defeat Jesus" team members feel a bit uncomfortable, but they indicate they will take part—if necessary—in this sinister plot. They realize Mr. Bigshot is proposing stepping over the line by suggesting committing a serious crime, but it's not like crime is a stranger to politics and the Democrat Party. The team again pledges its total commitment to defeating Rabbi Jesus and getting Lady Socialist elected.

Now the "Defeat Jesus" team is off and running full steam ahead! The blistering newspaper articles and horrendous TV news stories are almost unimaginable. The vitriol and smear campaign against Rabbi Jesus makes the bitter hostility toward President Trump look mild by comparison. The harsh rhetoric directed at the Rabbi is almost unconscionable—making the "fake news" media outlets seem like they had been handling Trump with kid gloves. But just as unbelievably, the Rabbi stays above the fray and continues to not only maintain His poll numbers but also increase in popularity. Rabbi Jesus has secured the Republican Party nomination. And Lady Socialist is the Democrat nominee, but her poll numbers haven't improved as much as the Democrats had hoped. The news media, and virtually everyone else, is shocked when Rabbi Jesus announces that He has selected a female Pentecostal preacher from Florida as His running mate. Nobody is surprised to learn that Lady Socialist also has selected a female vice-presidential running mate. The liberal media is thrilled by these announcements. They talk briefly about the lack of wisdom the Rabbi displays in selecting a female preacher as His running mate, but then they turn their attention to promoting the merits of having two females running the country. According to them, such an inept decision by Rabbi Jesus is sure to hand the presidency to Lady Socialist. The media is certain the United States will have its first-ever female president, and as an extra bonus—a female vice president! Great excitement is in the air and on the airwaves, and everyone is anxiously awaiting both the presidential and vice-presidential debates.

Lady Socialist stumbles during the first debate, while the Rabbi is well-prepared, cool, and confident. During one of the debates, when Rabbi Jesus is asked about His racism and lack of inclusion, He indicates that He loves everybody. The Rabbi's response surprises everyone when He says that He doesn't condemn anybody, but that He wants to be friends with everyone. All of the Rabbi's answers seem to include language about loving everyone; He spoke often of love and peace. He responded to many debate questions by quoting scriptures, and He also spoke in many parables that only certain conservative Christians seem to understand. The Rabbi made bold claims about changing the United States and the entire world for the good of all mankind. The debate moderators and liberal Democrat audience had difficulty understanding many of Rabbi Jesus' responses, but the conservative Christians expressed great enthusiasm.

The vice-presidential debates went pretty much the same, with Pentecostal Paula coming to the debates well-prepared and quoting various scriptures in response to many questions. Her opponent was not so well-prepared, and like Lady Socialist, she stumbled through some of her responses and was unable to make a good case for socialism to many potential voters.

The presidential debate commission decided to limit space for the Republican audience to only seven seats for the final debate. The debate team moderators were thrilled by this decision and commended the wisdom of the commission. Supporters for Rabbi Jesus were very disheartened, but the Rabbi assured them that He wasn't concerned about His limited audience. The Rabbi's seven Republican fans were loud and boisterous every time He responded to a question. They cheered loudly and enthusiastically. The moderators and Democrat audience were irritated by their enthusiasm. In fact, the Republicans had so much to cheer about that they overshadowed the Democrat audience and drowned out their attempted interference with the Rabbi's responses.

Following the final debate, news journalists immediately descended upon the two audiences to garner their comments about how their respective candidate fared and who won the debate. One female journalist smiled into the camera and announced, "Here are those two famous Hollywood brothers! One supports Lady Socialist, and the other Rabbi Jesus. Let's hear what they have to say and get their reactions to the debate." When asked by the news reporter who had won the debate, both brothers emphatically claimed their candidate had won. The younger brother was excited almost to the point of ecstasy about the potential of Rabbi Jesus becoming the next president of the United States. The elder brother had nothing but disdain for the Rabbi and called Him an enemy of the people and especially an adversary of Hollywood. According to him, virtually no one in the arts and entertainment world supported Rabbi Jesus. However the younger brother clearly was an adoring fan of the Rabbi and he pointed out His many admirable attributes. The journalist simply rolled her eyes and announced that she must move on. She thanked the elder brother for his insightful comments while essentially snubbing and showing contempt for his younger brother.

The "Defeat Jesus" team also was approached by journalists, but they didn't spend much time with the media. The team had major concerns to discuss and evaluate. The team had learned after the debate that Brandon Straka and his band of defectors had been invited to speak at the Rabbi's next political rally. And it had been reported that Rabbi Jesus had been hanging out with people from all walks of life, including the LGBTQ community. The Rabbi's most faithful Christian supporters and LGBTQs also were seen with each other—not just at campaign rallies but at other venues, greeting each other with warm embraces and high-fives. The progressives and Pharisees were truly panicked now. It was time to call an emergency meeting!

It was also time to implement the team's failsafe plan. Mr. Progressive Bigshot called on his most trusted allies, his small inner circle. One of the progressives agreed to allow her two young sons to be supposedly kidnapped. For the plan to be believable to a gullible public, the team decided to hold the boys for several days while a large-scale police investigation and public search ensued. The sons were turned over to a trusted team member who took them out of state and hid them in a secure location. Frantic Progressive Mom notified the police that her sons were missing and that she feared the worst. The story and the pictures of the boys were blasted all over the news. Frantic Mom held a press conference and put on a very good show, expressing what seemed to be real grief and begging whoever had taken her boys to release them.

The Lady Socialist campaign immediately got on board, also asking the kidnappers to return the boys. Rabbi Jesus, His campaign staff, and many of His supporters held prayer vigils for the boys. The Rabbi said that He believed the boys would be found quickly and unharmed. Sure enough, as the Rabbi predicted, the boys were found three days later—but not unharmed, according to them.

The young boys had been coached to accuse Rabbi Jesus of kidnapping and molesting them. Naturally, the Rabbi and His campaign staffers denied any wrongdoing, and many of His most-loyal supporters did not believe the boys. It was their word against His, so an extensive investigation would be conducted, and it was anybody's guess how long that would take. Although the Rabbi had been accused of this horrible crime, the police and most conservatives were reluctant to believe the progressives. They saw this as just another ploy by the Democrats to sabotage the Rabbi's campaign. But some conservatives and many Independents said they could no longer support the Rabbi's candidacy. Law enforcement had no other alternative but to arrest Rabbi Jesus. But after several days of questioning and comparing the stories of the seemingly traumatized boys and the clearly traumatized Rabbi, the police suspected foul play on the part of the Democrats. A Trump-appointed judge released Rabbi Jesus on a $500 million bond and instructed Him not to leave the country. The judge surprisingly also told the Rabbi to continue His campaign, while people everywhere were calling for Rabbi Jesus to suspend His campaign immediately. The Rabbi now had to face an even more hostile media and an extremely dangerous environment with people screaming for law enforcement officials to crucify Him.

Such a high-profile case caused the national director of the FBI to be called in to investigate. A full-scale investigation began, but the Rabbi was encouraged by His faithful supporters to remain in the race. The polls were no longer in favor of Rabbi Jesus. Pollsters now predicted with absolute confidence that Lady Socialist would win all fifty states in the general election. The plotting of the progressives and the Pharisees had worked! And the "Defeat Jesus" team was now firmly cemented together, although many members of the team still had no idea the kidnapping story was simply a hoax dreamed up by Mr. Bigshot and his inner circle. The team continued to embellish the merits of Lady Socialist, while impugning the character of Rabbi Jesus—which had been made much easier now that the Rabbi had been accused of pedophilia. Team members constantly articulated their disgust for Rabbi Jesus, while commending the political platform of Lady Socialist. All the conniving and the plotting of the failsafe plan would pay off when Lady Socialist was finally inaugurated as the president of the United States in January. In the meantime, there was still a general election to get through. Inwardly, Mr. Bigshot was very pleased with himself for contriving such a brilliant plan.

The plan had been successful in assassinating not only the character of Rabbi Jesus but also that of His Christian followers and the GOP. The team had no need to fabricate additional lies; they just needed to keep the big lie safe—the Rabbi's reputation had been ruined and His campaign was now on life support. Only His most devoted followers were still standing by and supplying Him with enough oxygen to barely stay in the race. Only the Bible-thumping, gun-clinging groups were still committed to the Rabbi, but they were clearly on a sinking ark.

Mr. Progressive Bigshot asked the "Defeat Jesus" team to keep up the unrelenting pressure on the Rabbi's campaign even though it was obviously now in ruins. All the major television media outlets, including CNN and MSNBC (with FOX News being a bit more reserved), booked numerous interviews with many progressives and Pharisees to discuss the horrific accusation against Rabbi Jesus. The news commentators were absolutely thrilled that the Rabbi had been accused of such a heinous crime. There was around-the-clock coverage with all regular programming suspended until after the general election. With a pious and sanctimonious attitude, Small Man Pharisee announced during an interview that he had always known the Rabbi was a phony and a menace to society. He also stated that the GOP was essentially dead, and that he would never vote for or associate with conservatives ever again. Other Pharisees chimed in that they were in full agreement with Small Man, and they considered themselves too holy to be connected with such a vile and beguiled political party. Many establishment Republicans were quick to condemn the Rabbi and indicate just how incensed they were that the GOP had been taken over by the right wing of the party. There was much weeping and repenting on the part of the *now-former* GOP members. The vehement hatred and distrust that the progressives, the Pharisees, and some establishment Republicans once had toward each other had now totally dissipated, and a trusting friendship had evolved between them. They pledged their total support to each other and to the defeat of Rabbi Jesus.

The Pharisees and establishment Republicans expressed to the television audience just how indecent the Rabbi truly was, how disgusted they were with His behavior, and how insulted they were by the GOP for endorsing Him. They proclaimed that He was now not only an alleged pedophile, but He had always been totally uncouth and was never a viable candidate for the presidency. The Pharisees reminded people how the Rabbi had once beaten a group of priests and physically driven them out of a synagogue—unconscionable! They also urged people to vote for the candidate who was committed to Baal worship and socialism! Surely Lady Socialist's promotion of Baal worship could not be as bad as the behavior of this man, Rabbi Jesus. The Pharisees also warned the television audience again that the Rabbi had whipped people, had spoken rudely, was a sexist and a racist, and had been accused of pedophilia. Then the Pharisees and establishment Republicans launched into a long discourse about Rabbi Jesus' posture on social issues, His obvious hypocritical attitude about Christianity, and how religious liberty was dangerously threatened by His positions. The Pharisees disclosed how they had completed a thorough search of the Rabbi's past, and things didn't look good for Him. And things looked a lot worse now in light of the serious accusation against Him. The Pharisees and their buddies on the left strongly denounced candidate Jesus.

The progressives also were anxious to divulge what they knew about the Rabbi's background. They discussed His lack of wisdom and foresight in choosing His friends, who were primarily uneducated, redneck bigots. And they explained to the viewers that only one of the Rabbi's associates seemed to have any common sense or sound judgment, but he had later been declared a traitor when he suddenly ended his friendship with the Rabbi. This former friend of Rabbi Jesus seemed to be the only person with a clear vision of who the Rabbi really was. Rabbi Jesus had evidently brainwashed most of His associates to further spread His religious propaganda. But most of these individuals were unstable individuals and traitors to their former religious faith. Small Man Pharisee then chimed in, "It seems Rabbi Jesus has made many poor decisions, and He has been affiliated with many questionable characters in the past. He has neither the political nor the spiritual acumen to run our country—or any country for that matter. Most establishment Republicans have never believed the Rabbi was a viable candidate; this is why, from the start, His candidacy was rejected by so many of us. He has also been known to collude with foreign countries, including that Far North country, against His own people's best interest. The Rabbi is capable of almost anything, and we believe the accusation of these precious young boys. He is a shameful disgrace to the GOP and the United States of America. Does anyone need further proof that Rabbi Jesus is a threat to Christianity and to our national security, and that His sexual orientation is a serious risk to our children? He is a malignancy that needs to be eradicated!" The progressives, the CNN commentator, and the Pharisees all nodded in agreement.

The CNN journalist then apologized profusely to the LGBTQ community for the actions of Rabbi Jesus, assuring them that no one blamed them for His despicable behavior. She stated that all of her friends were gays, lesbians, and transgender people, but there were many red flags concerning the Rabbi based on His past. The journalist explained further that it was not the intent of anyone on the panel to offend or injure the LGBTQ community in any way but rather, they intended to insult Rabbi Jesus. Then the journalist and everyone on the interview panel shifted nervously in their seats and giggled heinously. In unison, the panel members proclaimed their intent was to warn the American people of how devilish the Rabbi was and how out of touch He was with American citizens and their values. Wall-to-wall, 24/7 coverage of the Rabbi's background and alleged crime continued to be broadcast on every network. In the meantime, wise Christians—known as the "remnant"—prayed, continually asking for God's intervention. That was something the progressives, establishment Republicans, and Pharisees didn't count on! And that was their mistake—as God answers the prayers of His faithful people.

FBI agents again gently questioned the young boys who had accused Rabbi Jesus of molesting them. Suddenly the story broke down, and first one and then the other boy confessed that the whole thing was a hoax! They began to cry, and then they explained how they had been coached by adults to accuse the Rabbi of wrongdoing—for a very good cause, they had been told. The boys had innocently gone along with the scheme, until it started interfering with their favorite TV programs, which had been taken off the air in order to provide 24/7 coverage of the Rabbi fiasco. Naturally, law enforcement held an immediate press conference clearing Rabbi Jesus but indicating they would be pursuing other arrests in the case.

Tomorrow will be general election day!

As the results started coming in on election night, the progressives were still confident that their candidate would win all fifty states by a landslide. But intentionally, no races were called until after the polls closed in California. And, as might be expected, all networks announced that Lady Socialist had won the great State of California—every county and all fifty-five electoral votes! The mood in the newsrooms was euphoric. But a short time later, their optimism turned to shock and disbelief, as state after state fell into the column for Rabbi Jesus. Journalists from CNN, MSNBC, CBS, NBC, ABC, and even a few folks at FOX News could be heard and seen weeping and wailing loudly. Rabbi Jesus had won the election and would be the next president of the United States! The Rabbi had won forty-nine of the fifty states, and the results in both the popular and electoral votes weren't even close. Riots broke out all over the United States by disgruntled voters. People fell on the sidewalks and in the streets, shaking their fists toward heaven and shouting obscenities at Rabbi Jesus, His followers, and almighty God.

Wait a minute—there is breaking news from CNN! The CNN commentator excitedly said, "The state of Florida has just announced that literally boxes and boxes of mail-in ballots, not formally counted, have been found in a storeroom. The votes come from heavily Democrat districts. And now we have another announcement coming in: Boxes and boxes of uncounted votes have also been found in Georgia, in Texas, in Missouri, in Ohio, in Kentucky, in Tennessee, in Virginia, in South Dakota, and in Michigan! Hold on, folks, literally what may amount to millions of uncounted votes from heavily Democratic districts have been found in forty-nine of the fifty states! This election is not over by a long shot!"

The journalists were now shouting for joy. CNN announced that Donald Trump was clearly wrong once again—America would be a socialist country after all!

The Christians immediately called for prayer vigils, and they vowed not to allow these newly found illegal votes to be counted. They were confident that Rabbi Jesus had won the election. God was on their side and would give them the victory. This sentiment was expressed over and over again by conservative Christians for the next several weeks. But the results of the election had become so distorted and compromised that the case must go to the now conservatively loaded Supreme Court to determine the final outcome. Commentators from MSNBC, CNN, and most of the other networks remained confident. And they reminded their audiences that even if Lady Socialist should be defeated, the Rabbi certainly would be impeached, since He clearly was not mentally competent to govern the country. They assured their television audience that impeachment proceedings would begin immediately should the Rabbi be declared the winner.

Most journalists from all the networks suddenly became absolutely giddy; they'd just learned about another even more progressive candidate who had been waiting in the shadows. His name was Lucifer Antichrist, and he was guaranteed to win the presidency in four years—four very short or very long years depending on one's perspective! The journalists assured their viewers that Lucifer Antichrist would be the most wonderful candidate ever to set foot on the political stage in the United States of America. He had a mesmerizing appeal, and the whole world stood in complete awe of him. Journalists at MSNBC, CNN, and most of the other news outlets were leaping, dancing, twirling, and shouting for joy, while some of the journalists at FOX News were weeping uncontrollably in anguish and disbelief. Chants could be heard in the newsrooms and from people in the streets, with animated awe and delirious excitement—"Lucifer, Lucifer, Lucifer Antichrist, Lucifer Antichrist, Lucifer Antichrist!"

CHAPTER 8

Radicals in Charge

I have set before you life and death,
blessing and cursing; therefore choose life,
that both you and your descendants may live.
DEUTERONOMY 30:19 NKJV

If Jesus were an actual candidate for president of the United States, would He really be the recipient of so much hatred, malice, and resistance from radicals, and could a scenario as outlined in the previous chapter be possible? I not only believe it is possible, but I believe it's actually *probable*! I'm confident the radical left would use no restraint in opposing Jesus. On the other hand, the Antichrist would be warmly welcomed in their circles. I used to question how anyone could be foolish enough or deceived enough to accept the Antichrist, but after the successful elections of so many radical politicians in recent elections, that question has forever been removed from my mind. After the election of President Obama, I realized that people, including many deceived Christians, not only support radical political positions, but someday will likely defend the Antichrist when he finally appears on the national stage—especially if he's an avowed far-left progressive.

Obama was hailed by many of his supporters as the greatest presidential candidate ever, and the greatest president ever, and he was even exalted by some to the lofty position of "messiah."

This was a grievous thing to followers of the true Messiah. To Obama's credit, he seemed reluctant and a bit embarrassed to be labeled as the messiah in this way. But his adoring fans bestowed the title on him anyway. Yet President Obama appeared to be the most anti-Christ president ever and the most eager to implement policies in direct violation of God's Word. This was a great source of grief to *true* followers of Christ. Although Obama claimed to know the Lord, his actions certainly didn't indicate that he did. He attended a social-justice church where radical ideology was preached, but the sermons were short on theology. Obama did throw his radical pastor under the bus, however, once he became a liability. This could be viewed as either good or bad, depending on one's point of view. Though it's not normally viewed favorably to show disloyalty to one's pastor, it's also not wise to remain in a black liberation-theology church—where an individual is unlikely to have a born-again experience.

President Obama was the most liberal president ever elected in our country; his ideology was radical, and he seemed determined to fundamentally change the United States forever. In fact, he stated on more than one occasion that he planned to fundamentally transform the United States. People who voted for him also evidently wanted to see the demise of our old values and the remaking of a new America. Obama and his enamored fans instinctively knew something was wrong in the United States. What they couldn't seem to grasp was that the problem was actually progressives like themselves who were trying to reshape the country to fit their radical worldview.

As progressive as Obama's ideology was, however, it apparently didn't go far enough to the left for many Democrats today. They keep pushing the envelope further left every day, presumably trying to fix the problems their progressive agenda was instrumental in creating in the first place—or trying to fix things that only they imagine are broken. Democrats refuse to accept that their radical ideology is the problem—and that it is responsible for generating problems rather than solving them. Their ideology is continuing to slide so far left that soon Nancy Pelosi, Chuck Schumer, and Barack Obama may appear moderate or even conservative by comparison.

Progressive politicians are attempting to drive our country over a cliff, while ungodly individuals cheer them onward! The cliff is visible; disaster is looming; but delusional Democrats and liberal Republicans see no danger—except for Trump. They are much more committed to launching attacks against President Trump and defeating his conservative agenda than they are about addressing important issues such as soaring crime rates in major cities they control like Chicago and Baltimore, and other Democrat-controlled cities like Los Angeles and San Francisco being overwhelmed by illegal immigration. (As a side note, this tweet by Les Dunaway tells the story in a clear, succinct manner: "San Francisco—Where the Dogs Step in Human Poop!")[8]

On any given weekend, the number of shootings in Chicago and Baltimore (especially in black-on-black crime) is staggering. Over long holiday weekends, the situation worsens. The statistics in certain sections of Chicago are particularly grim due to gang violence. It's not unusual for the city to record five to eight or more murders in a weekend, along with numerous non-fatal shootings. The typical newspaper headlines for the Windy City read: "Seven fatally shot, and forty-three injured by gunfire." Baltimore typically has fewer murders and shootings over the same weekend, but only because its population is much smaller than the city of Chicago. So, in reality, Baltimore is the more violent city—even though fewer people are killed weekly or annually in Charm City. NeighborhoodScout indicates that Baltimore is more dangerous than Chicago, as are a lot of other cities based on violent-crime victims per 1,000 residents, and it also states that Chicago **is not** the murder capital of the United States, as some suppose. At the same time, Chicago has mass shootings by numerous villains virtually every weekend. These shootings are largely ignored, while a mass shooting by a single nonminority perpetrator receives lots of media coverage and loud outcries from politicians at the federal level pushing gun control.

Violent crime in cities such as Memphis, Birmingham, St. Louis, Kansas City, and Detroit—to name only a few—also goes essentially unnoticed by most liberal politicians. Somehow the mean streets of Baltimore, Chicago, Memphis, Detroit, and numerous other cities across the country have escaped the attention of Democrat mayors and other liberal bureaucrats. The problems in many of these cities have been exacerbated by the large influx of illegal immigrants, many of whom are homeless and live out on the mean streets. Another issue that has contributed to the crime problem in the United States is substance abuse, which has led to turf wars and an escalation in gang activity. None of this moves liberals, though; their sole focus is suppressing anything the president desires to do to remedy any of these undesirable situations. Evidently, liberal politicians fear his policies may effect a positive outcome that they themselves should have made happen years ago.

In their heightened state of paranoia, liberal politicians appear unaware of much else but Trump, and they never offer anything remotely resembling constructive solutions for real issues. Their uncompromising, unyielding, and belligerent behavior toward our president, commonly referred to by conservatives as *Trump Derangement Syndrome*, makes liberals abandon all logic in order to adopt irrational opposition to anything proposed by the Trump administration. Their problem-solving initiatives have been reduced to Trump-bashing, and real solutions have been abandoned in favor of redefining words and concepts to conform to their radical ideology.

Liberals are far more interested in changing gender-specific terms to politically correct, gender-neutral language than they are in solving real problems in the country. Getting rid of gender-specific terms has become a major issue for liberals, along with, of course, changing the rules as to who is allowed to use ladies' restrooms and locker rooms or who can compete in women's sports. What could possibly rise to the level of importance of changing *manhole* to *maintenance hole*, or using the gender-neutral title "Mx" when addressing transgender individuals or those wishing to remain gender nonspecific, or allowing biological males to identify as females? Liberals and other radicals appear to be convinced that these and similar issues are of the utmost importance for the advancement and survival of our culture. They're also convinced that white males represent a real threat to society, that white privilege and racism are rampant in the United States, that guns kill people, that more diversity is needed in politics and corporate America, that red baseball caps are terrifying, and that President Trump and his conservative supporters are contemptible degenerates to be greatly feared—and the list goes on and on.

To take a page from Dylan Wheeler's *Educating Liberals* playbook, I will attempt to provide my own educational insight regarding these issues. Most white males do not pose a threat to any of us, especially conservative white males. On the other hand, liberal males of any hue are scary! I saw a liberal black CNN journalist once expressing the grave danger white males represent to the nation. Incredibly, his liberal white male cohost agreed with him. The black journalist is married to a white male; this makes me wonder if the CNN journalist sleeps with one eye open! Also, liberals would have us believe that white privilege is automatically bestowed on all white people at birth, and that whites should be ashamed and apologize to *people of color* for our privileged status! Well, I, like many other people, was born white—and into abject poverty. I can say with complete honesty that white privilege never came knocking at my door!

With permission, I'm including in this chapter an article on "White Privilege" written by my niece, Bobbi Wilson of Monroe, Ohio.

Response to Hillary Clinton's White Privilege Nonsense

Recently Hillary Clinton called out to white Americans to recognize and apologize to African Americans for, and I quote, "Our White Privilege."

Well, needless to say, I, as a white American, am steamed! Not at the intelligent, all great, and powerful Hillary, oh no, not at her. I'm steamed—in fact, I am outraged—at the stupidity of my ignorant, white-cracker parents—the two people I call Mom and Dad! I cannot for one second believe the injustice that these two have bestowed upon me! I mean, can you believe the injustice done to me by these two sight-gifted individuals who obviously realized on the day I was born, back in July 1975, that I was a "white" baby. There wasn't a question about my color; it wasn't like I was just light-skinned or even a high-yellow—no, I was clearly as white as white can be. Heck, even the doctor checked the "white" box on my birth certificate!

But still, these dumb jerks didn't bother checking me out of the hospital through the "White Privilege" line. Oh no, these idiots just checked me out alongside all the other average, everyday American-born babies.

Now, after listening to Ms. Hillary, I realize how wrong my parents were! And just think, I could have grown up in one of those big houses—you know—the ones with the pool inside and the tennis court outside. I could have been spending my cool spring days taking private tennis lessons from Andre Agassi, while my governess—who would have most likely been Mary flipping Poppins—was bringing me fresh-squeezed lemonade to quench my parched little throat. And this was only after she finished wiping my behind, cleaning my room, and running my bubble bath! My summers would have been spent sailing on my yacht to exotic lands like the Galapagos Islands, and then over to the Great Barrier Reef for some leisurely snorkeling. My winter break? Well, heck, I'm sure it would have been spent in the Swiss Alps—where, after a long day of skiing, my family and I would have retired to the lodge, sat around the big, crackling fireplace, and had a butler serve us hot chocolate. By the time I was eighteen, I would have been so well-rounded, well-traveled, and well-educated that Harvard Law School would have gladly opened its doors to me on a full-ride scholarship. And by now, I would have become an extremely wealthy and successful attorney—maybe even the U.S. Attorney General.

Not only did my parents fail to check me out through the "White Privilege" line, but these stupid jerks also lied to me! They started their silver-tongued lies right from jump street—with crap like "nothing in life is free"; followed up by "hard work pays off"; "the early bird gets the worm"; "if you are going to do something, do it right or don't do it at all"; "life isn't fair"; and "you have to respect your parents, elders, and people of authority"! I mean to tell you, the lies just kept coming! Thank God for Hillary, or I would *still* be in the dark!

But you want to know what really chaps my behind? Not only did they lie and not only did they not give me the "White Privilege" that I so richly deserved (my birthright!)—but these two idiots didn't even tell me about it! I had to get this information from Hillary Clinton! So now at forty, I have four children who also were not checked out of the hospital correctly. And they won't graduate from Harvard—they will have to take out college loans; work hard for their degrees; stay out of trouble; show respect to authority figures; get a job; pay taxes; and follow the law.

Gee, thanks a lot Mom and Dad. Because of the way you raised me, I am exactly who I am today! So, I apologize, I really do! I apologize to all the African Americans for not being raised black and for not being raised white—but for my two parents who raised me right!

Note: I think Bobbi really nailed it with this article! *White privilege* is an invention of the left used to pander to minority voters. What many minority voters don't realize is that a lot of whites growing up in America, during a long period of our history, were very poor, with little or no food to satisfy their hunger. I can remember numerous occasions when there was no food at our house, and I went to bed hungry. This doesn't describe "privilege," but "underprivileged" to me.

While liberals see the United States as unjust and whites as privileged, conservatives see things much differently. I don't deny that privilege exists, especially privilege for the rich and famous and corrupt politicians—without regard to race. Privilege is undeniably experienced by liberal politicians and many other celebrities, extending even to the realm of justice. Laws applying to ordinary citizens frequently don't apply to them, and the laws are conveniently overlooked or ignored completely. It's truly rare to see corrupt politicians and celebrities convicted of their crimes. They're normally exempt from retribution.

White privilege and equitable justice are only imagined, and they don't exist for ordinary citizens of the country. Also, the shameful racism that's running rampant in the United States, according to liberals, is largely imagined. The white racists I know are all liberals!

Now, to the next subject that alarms liberals—guns! According to liberals, guns of their own accord kill people. Yet I've never seen a single gun shoot anybody without a person first pulling the trigger, unless the gun is dropped by an individual and somehow it goes off accidently. Blaming guns only shifts the blame from the person responsible to an inanimate object that cannot kill anyone on its own accord.

Another subject that appears to be continually on the radar screens of liberals is that of a perceived lack of diversity. They're always clamoring for more diversity. On the issue of more diversity, how diverse must a political party or organization be to satisfy liberals? I used to live in Virginia near Washington, D.C. Diversity was a big liberal issue in D.C. In some government offices, in particular, there was so much diversity that there was no diversity; all the employees were minorities. I like to call these organizations *overachievers*. They meet their quotas for diversity and then some! In July 2019, top white female staffers employed by the Democratic Congressional Campaign Committee (DCCC), along with some of their white male coworkers, were essentially forced to resign their positions due to a "lack of diversity" in key positions at the DCCC; this was after most of us had been convinced by liberals that females were off-limits. Liberal concern for diversity in politics generally only applies as it relates to conservatives. White males are still very prominent in the Democrat Party, even at the top of the ticket! At times, there's a lot of noise about the inappropriateness of white males running for president in this modern age of enlightenment, but then the commotion dies down—and there's almost deafening silence on the subject! But the hypocrisy is loud and clear.

Apparently, based on the ethnicity of many of the 2020 Democrat presidential hopefuls, white males ignored their own liberal doctrine. Did they not read the full-page progressive memo instructing them that white is bad; white is privileged; and in order to promote fairness, white males ought to be relegated to the bottom of the food chain to make way for women and minorities? Evidently, these men are not "woke," like so many other radical Democrats and feminists—or perhaps they're hypocritically ignoring their own "wokeness." It makes one wonder why there have been no ANTIFA or Black Lives Matter protests and no liberal Hollywood speeches condemning the audacity and hypocrisy of these men. But perhaps someday soon, these white males will realize that they're relics of the past, soon to be demoted to the position of under-rowers on their own progressive ship. Surely, the politics of liberalism will one day *soon* demand it—white males disavowed!

Liberals are a mystifying people group. They seem to be continually redefining themselves and their beliefs as they also redefine perfectly logical words or terms to fit their ever-changing, utterly perplexing, and ever-progressively unsound ideology. Soon the very reliable *Webster's Dictionary* may have to be replaced by the *Liberal Dictionary of Modern English Language* to help people keep up with current definitions. A negative side effect of all this change seems to be overloading the brains of many liberals. Constant change appears to be affecting their short-term memories. In fact, the changes come so frequently that maybe a *Liberalism Dictionary* would be too labor-intensive to successfully manage. Liberals in politics, and the media in particular, seem to suffer from a phenomenon that I call *change overload*, often causing them to forget what they believed only yesterday. I'm convinced that many liberals in Hollywood also suffer from *change overload* as well as *Botox brain*. Celebrities in Hollywood are literally poisoning their brains with facial Botox injections, so it's no wonder that many of them not only look unnatural, but also exhibit bizarre behavior.

Some liberals, particularly in Hollywood, are now absolutely traumatized by red baseball caps (possibly annoying effects of

Botox brain?). Who knew that red baseball caps could be so terrifying! To some unstable individuals, these caps somehow represent evil, and MAGA hats completely incapacitate liberals. Their fear is imagined, but it's real to them. I won't be surprised when liberals and other fanatical extremists eventually insist on banning the color *red* altogether. After all, red represents MAGA, President Trump, Trump supporters, and conservative states in America. In fact, red represents most of the United States. Election results show every cycle just how red most of the United States really is, and how little blue appears on the geographical map. Without the support of large liberal, metropolitan areas of the country, Democrats would never win a single election. Oh, and as a very important side note, red also represents the blood of Jesus Christ. I'm happy that red still covers most of the United States!

Conservatives terrify liberals and other radicals, because those on the left don't realize it's conservatives who prevent them from driving the country completely over a cliff. They don't understand that conservatives are the only protective barrier, or safety net, standing between them and total devastation. Radical extremists foolishly oppose conservatives and deem them evil. They see conservatives and Christians as enemies to be feared; they view prayer as problematic, and they consider the Bible to be hate speech. Hatred propels them to regard followers of Christ as intolerant bigots or even domestic terrorists. But it is radicals who, in reality, are intolerant and are terrorizing the country. They express contempt for anyone who disagrees with their radical doctrine; only conservatives prevent total mayhem.

Liberals remain in a perpetual state of fear and a continuous pursuit of power because they believe it's up to them to save the world—from global warming (which they have imagined), from racial and income inequality (which they have created), from hate speech (which they have invented), and most of all, from conservative thought! Ungodly folks are convinced their purpose is to save the planet from extinction. They're persuaded that, in order to save the world, they must first defeat conservatism. This not only gives them cause to fear, but also a voracious appetite for power. Liberals are relentless in their pursuit of power in order to keep what they regard as ignorant conservative dissidents from power. They are a detriment to themselves and a grave danger to the rest of society.

Liberal and far-left politicians will injure opponents and damage anyone's reputation to gain or stay in power for a few more days or even just a few more hours. These politicians don't care whom they hurt or destroy in the process. Their thirst for power is so insatiable that they're willing to sell their souls for just one more hour! Irresponsible journalists, supercilious celebrities, and other ungodly people, along with uninformed voters, help them fulfill their lust, while inflicting great damage on our country and our culture.

Arrogant politicians, along with their devout followers, want to completely transform the United States of America. They want to change America, because they hate America and view it as an abhorrent evil. These unscrupulous politicians and their avid fans want a country without secure borders, without law and order, and without the Lord Jesus Christ. They want to reshape and remake the United States into a profane image, an image that is clueless, careless, ruthless, reckless, lawless, and godless. Somehow, they believe everyone will be happier once the United States is remade and reduced to a destitute third-world socialist or communist country. Then and only then will we find utopia and be happy. Total desolation is the ultimate goal for America.

These politicians and their committed followers reside in a very dark place spiritually, but their deceptive hearts convince them that they're the righteous saviors of our country and the whole universe. The Bible says in Jeremiah 17:9, "The heart is deceitful above all things, and desperately wicked; who can know it?" These individuals, politicians and voters alike, do not realize that their hearts are lying to them and cheating them out of God's purpose for their lives. There's a country-and-western song performed by the great Hank Williams Sr. called "Your Cheatin' Heart." The lyrics say, "Your cheatin' heart will tell on you." Putting a spiritual spin on this sad love song, if liberals would acknowledge the Lord—their cheating hearts would tell on them and they would be converted. But because they continue to oppose God, their hearts continue to deceive them, causing them to accept evil and reject that which is good. This is the reason so many liberals resist President Trump's conservative agenda, while promoting radical ideology.

President Trump, once considered a liberal himself, is now seen as a tremendous threat to liberalism. His policies are perceived as an attempt to change the liberal culture that currently permeates our society. This explains much of the hostile resistance by liberals toward him and his political agenda—and the consistent furor about things he hasn't done or hasn't said. Psalm 56:5 says, "All day they twist my words; all their thoughts are against me for evil." This scripture perfectly describes the unreasonable animosity toward President Trump and his family. Deceitful people frequently state things that our president supposedly has said that didn't even come close to the reality of what he actually communicated. They are twisting his words because their thoughts are evil against him and their deceitful hearts lie to them and make them hear things that were never spoken.

Deceitful hearts lead to all sorts of problematic issues, and they breed opposition to good, while endorsing evil. This is why we cannot ever allow radical politicians to gain complete control over our government. If that ever happens, our country will be dismantled, our freedoms torpedoed, and our most cherished institutions obliterated. Then the future will indeed be bleak for us and future generations. We will be relegated to a godless country that is no longer recognizable with elected officials who don't represent the values of the majority of us. The consequences will be dire, and the fault will lie largely at the feet of misguided Christians who vote foolishly or who don't bother to vote at all! Some Christians won't vote for either party, but they're *closet* Democrats. These people I refer to as *Democrat sympathizers*. They secretly despise conservatives, and they covertly adore radicals. They know the Lord doesn't approve of anyone actively supporting the ungodly Democrat theology, so they don't vote at all—secretly hoping the Democrats will win. In this manner, they're able to appease their consciences and at the same time fool themselves, but they don't fool God who knows their thoughts and understands the motives of their cheating hearts.

The people of God should be fully engaged in choosing suitable officials who can be trusted to govern our country with Christian ethics. Our politicians don't necessarily have to be Christians, but we shouldn't elect those who are hostile toward Christ. It's amazing how many politicians suddenly become religious when it's considered expedient for them to do so; it's also astonishing how many gullible people fall for this lie. One presidential hopeful in 2020 supposedly quoted her favorite Bible verse; there's just one problem—there is no such Bible verse. Perhaps she's quoting from her own version of a Bible; a Bible she has authored herself! It's a bit surprising to hear her and other Democrat candidates trying to quote scripture, but then this is done to pander to naïve Christians who are also unable to quote a single scripture correctly themselves. One seriously deluded candidate claimed that abortion is sanctioned by the Bible!

It still may be beneficial today for liberal politicians to claim allegiance to Christ, but I believe the day is soon coming when it will no longer be profitable for them to do so. In fact, it will be considered by many, and probably all in the Democrat Party, to be a liability. And when politicians are asked if they are persons of faith and believe in Jesus Christ, the answer will be a resounding *no—not now and not ever!* As the country and politics become more and more secular, it will be unacceptable for anyone in the Democrat Party to support a man or woman of faith, especially one who is truly dedicated to Christ. Many Democrats already consider a person of faith to be intolerant and unsuitable for public office. Unless there is a sweeping change in the spiritual welfare of our country, people professing Christ will be rejected as viable political candidates by the Democrat Party. Currently, we have several Christians serving in the Trump administration—an encouraging sign for the spiritual health of our nation. The tide may finally be turning in the right direction, but the question is, *how much longer will it last?* To keep the country moving forward spiritually, the president needs *all* conservatives and Christians to support him, his agenda, and his administration, and abandon liberal politicians and their radical political platform.

Christians in particular need to be actively involved not only in the Great Commission, but also in politics. We need to be fully on board with President Trump and his agenda. And we need to become radically engaged in the advancement of conservative ideas and godly principles in our country. The word *radical* was once a good term that was applied to Republicans who were fighting to end slavery and promote civil rights. Conservatives, especially Christians, need to make the word *radical* good again. Imagine residing in a country where *radical* is applied once again in a positive way to Christians and Christianity. The radical Republicans in the 1800s believed that black Americans were entitled to the same political rights and opportunities as whites, and they worked to implement civil rights for former slaves. Now, that's being radical for the good of others! Christians and conservatives today need to become known as radically good, promoting morality and integrity.

It's up to us, the citizens of the United States, to determine what kind of country we desire to live in and what type of political system we want to be governed by. I sincerely hope most of us want a country with honest elections, a country where we won't be ostracized for our Christian beliefs, a country where we have secure borders, financial security, respect for law and order, and freedom of speech. I also hope the majority of us want a country that protects the civil rights of *all* citizens, a country where justice applies equally to all, and where religious and political freedoms are valued. I genuinely hope we want a country where political coups will never be attempted again, or if attempted, where the wicked perpetrators will be brought to justice—not allowing them to go unpunished, as is the case today.

With the election of President Trump, evil people tried to make a mockery of our election system. If we want to remain a free and open society, we cannot allow this to happen in our country with impunity. We cannot permit villains, whether politicians or not, whether celebrities or not, to go unpunished. We also cannot allow crooked politicians, pompous celebrities, "fake news" journalists, and others like them to scam and deceive us. It's time for us to vote radicals out of office and take back our country while there is still a country to be rescued. Again, if we are foolish enough to let radicals dictate what our country should be, then we will lose our beloved nation and our way of life. I hope *all* conservatives will take decisive action now and not wait for tomorrow. If we ever allow the radical left to be totally in charge, then the battle will be lost and all of us will go over the cliff together, or we'll be like those on the *Titanic*—singing hymns as the ship is going down!

God truly smiled upon us when He gave us a great gift in the presidency of Donald Trump—a gift that much of the nation doesn't deserve or appreciate. Unfortunately, there are still far too many corrupt politicians and liberal unelected officials in our government who need to be replaced by conservatives, and far too many dishonest journalists who need to be superseded by conservative voices.

It's easy to identify corrupt politicians: They're dishonest, often angry, disobedient to authority, and project radical points of view. We must be proactive and vote these individuals out of office, and then we must expose corrupt unelected officials so they, too, can be removed from their positions. And we must stop watching the liberal "fake news" networks and get our news from conservative sources instead. My husband and I watch local news and FOX almost exclusively, but there are many news commentators on FOX whom we also refuse to watch. We did watch the 2016 election results on several news networks, because the liberals were just so entertaining. We still occasionally pull up the 2016 election night coverage—the best night of entertainment in the history of network television! The frantic reactions of liberal pundits and commentators are so hilarious. We get a fun-filled night of entertainment at their expense, and we don't even need popcorn!

But beware, even after the election of President Trump, radicals are still out to wreck our country and annihilate our freedoms. Unless we take aggressive action now to elect true conservatives, the country still remains on a dangerous course.

People who are spiritually awake realize that if radicals ever gain complete control of our government or other valued institutions, our country will be gone forever—never to be resurrected! We cannot let that happen. We must take decisive action to defeat radicals at the ballot box, in newspaper press rooms, on college campuses, and behind broadcast news desks! To have a healthy country and a bright future, they must be replaced *by us!*

If we remain sensitive to the Holy Spirit, He will reveal leaders to us of whom He approves, those who embrace a biblical worldview, who won't meddle in foreign elections, and who won't start unnecessary wars. We must learn to follow the Lord's guidance in choosing political representatives. In the past, we've elected a few good officials, some mediocre ones, but far too many incompetent leaders, because we failed to seek God's counsel and elect His choice. Let's learn from the past, and use caution, wisdom, and foresight to choose the right leaders to govern us in the future.

CHAPTER 9

Bad Kings, Good Kings, and the Perfect King

I will establish him in My house and in My kingdom forever; and his throne shall be established forever.

1 CHRONICLES 17:14 NKJV

Historically, people have failed to choose the right kind of leadership to represent them. This is true here in the United States, as it is in other nations around the world. We are fortunate to live in a country where we are given the privilege to vote in *supposedly* free and open elections, although *free and open* has come into question as of late. I believe it's not only a right, but the duty of every citizen to vote in local, state, and federal elections. It's also the duty of Christians to research the candidates and issues, and to vote wisely to make their votes count on the side of righteousness.

Christians can't expect leaders to be perfect, but they should make every effort to elect individuals who honor their values and respect their beliefs. There are no perfect, or even nearly perfect, politicians. A search for perfection is futile and only leads to disappointment. In the course of human history, there has been only one perfect King—the Lord Jesus Christ! The leadership of even the best politician pales in comparison to that of the only perfect King, but we shouldn't allow this to discourage us from voting, nor should we be swayed by all the negative political rhetoric. We must be wise enough to separate facts from fiction. For years, evil men and women have been trying to highjack our elections and those of other countries to defeat godly leadership. Clearly, there are leaders of whom God approves, and other rulers of whom He disapproves. We need discernment to know the difference. We must attempt to select leaders of whom our perfect King approves, hopefully, those with a biblical worldview, or at least those who aren't hostile to Christ and Christianity. We must be led by the Holy Spirit.

We must never allow ourselves to be fooled by liberal politicians quoting Bible verses out of context, nor should we be fooled by the media endorsing liberal candidates. We cannot permit ourselves to be deceived by *fake news* stories and *conspiracy* theories. We must be mature enough and become informed enough to see politics and politicians from God's perspective. To be mature and informed, we must learn to have our senses trained to discern good and evil. See Hebrews 5:14. We absolutely cannot rely on the media to give us an honest evaluation of a politician's position on important issues, nor a political party's ideology. Christians in particular need never be confused or deceived by politicians. We can ask God for His direction. We can search the New Testament for guidance, and we can also gain insight by studying the history of ancient Israel and its leaders in the Old Testament. If we study the history of Israel's leaders, we will gain an understanding of leadership from God's perspective, and we will also realize that we can't expect perfect human leaders. The Bible reveals that most leaders don't accomplish God's purposes on earth very well, but the best leaders are those specifically chosen by God—rather than by people. This was clearly true in ancient Israel, and it's still true today.

Let's take a look at the history of ancient Israel before the perfect King, Jesus, arrived on the scene. The Bible reveals that God initially chose leaders such as Moses and Joshua to lead Israel. Later, ancient Israel was ruled first by judges and then by a few good kings, but primarily bad kings. The Israelites were also subject to foreign kings after disobeying God and going into captivity; they were governed by several empires, including the

Assyrians, the Babylonians, the Medes-Persians, the Greeks, and the Romans. They were under Roman rule when Jesus appeared in Israel. The Bible gives a fairly extensive account of our perfect King and various kings reigning over Israel during biblical times. Unlike modern Israel today, the people in ancient Israel didn't have the privilege of choosing their leaders through a general election process.

The Old Testament provides a relatively detailed history of numerous kings ruling over God's chosen people. Most people are familiar with at least a few of the more famous kings. Even secular people probably have heard of King David (a man after God's own heart) and his son King Solomon (the wisest and richest man to ever live), and perhaps King Ahab (one of the most evil kings to rule over Israel). If people aren't familiar with King Ahab, they've probably heard of his wicked wife, Queen Jezebel.

All of us, if we're wise, desire good kings or presidents to represent us and lead us. But some of us often find it difficult to differentiate between good and bad kings when applying God's standards. This is particularly true if we view leaders strictly from a human or natural perspective. So, I thought it might be helpful to take a look at some of the kings listed in the Old Testament to learn what made them good or bad based on God's point of view.

First, let's take a look at the first king of Israel—King Saul—then we'll move on to King David and his son King Solomon. After these three kings, we'll look at the kings who ruled once the kingdom was divided and became the northern kingdom of Israel and the southern kingdom of Judah. For a more detailed history of the kings of Israel and Judah, read 1 and 2 Samuel, 1 and 2 Kings, and 1 and 2 Chronicles.

King Saul was the first Israelite king to rule over the land of Israel. Prior to Saul, God's people were ruled by judges. Probably the most famous judge and one whom many people are familiar with was Samuel. Samuel was a very godly man. He had been dedicated to the Lord as a young child. Samuel's mother, Hannah, had been unable to have a child (which was considered a curse in those days), and so she went to the court of the tabernacle to pray for a son, which she promised to give back to the Lord if He answered her prayer. Not surprisingly, God did answer her prayer. True to her word, when Samuel was a very young child, Hannah took him to the tabernacle and left him with Eli, the priest, to be trained up in the admonition of the Lord. After Samuel grew up, he judged and ruled until he was an old man, and then his sons took over his role. Unlike Samuel, his sons were ungodly men. The Israelites demanded a king; they wanted to be led by a king, like the other nations around them that were ruled by a king. Having a king at that time to rule the people was not God's idea, but He acquiesced and allowed Israel to have a king. God instructed Samuel to warn the people that they would be unhappy with King Saul, that he would take advantage of them. The people rebelliously ignored God's warning and demanded that they be given a king anyway, so God honored their request.

King Saul was not a "God idea," but a "people idea"! King Saul started out small and humble, but he soon became arrogant and disobedient to the Lord. And he greatly disappointed the people. He started out well, but he ended very badly. It's not as important how one starts as it is how one finishes. King Saul also was plagued with jealousy toward David, and he tried to kill him numerous times. Saul even gave his daughter Michal, who was David's wife, to another man to wed. His foolishness eventually led to his death and the premature death of his sons who were fighting in battle with him, one of whom was David's best friend, Jonathan. (In spite of Saul's bad behavior, David remained a loyal friend to Jonathan and later showed great kindness to Jonathan's son and King Saul's grandson Mephibosheth.) As God predicted, King Saul was a complete disaster! (Lesson: When choosing your leaders, ask God for His advice!)

After the death of Saul, his son Ishbosheth (Esh-Baal) became king over Israel—again not God's idea—and King David was anointed king over Judah. Eventually, David became king over all of Israel. Unlike Saul, David *was* God's idea. David was chosen by God and loved dearly by the Lord. King David became known as a man after God's heart, even though he was a very flawed man. David was a lousy husband and father, plus he essentially stole another man's wife and then had him murdered. (Wow, and David was God's choice!) God didn't allow David to go unpunished for his sins, and He disciplined him gravely. The Lord told King David that trouble and turmoil would never depart from his house as long as he lived. As I stated previously, David was an extremely imperfect human being. He had multiple wives—not unusual for the culture at the time—but he also took his wife Michal away from her new husband (the one to whom her father, King Saul, had given her). Both Michal and her husband were devastated at David's action. It's fairly evident from the biblical account that neither David nor Michal still loved each other. It appears that David saw Michal as his property, so he simply reclaimed what was his. They never shared an intimate relationship after David reclaimed her. Then there is the issue of one of David's sons raping his half-sister and David failing to discipline him. Another of David's sons later killed the half-brother, then revolted and tried to overthrow David and replace him as king. The Bible presents rather shocking details of King David's life. The Bible reflects the good, the bad, and the ugly. Given the story of David's life, it makes one wonder why the Lord was so fond of him. But King David was a great lover and worshiper of God. He is identified as the writer of at least seventy-three of the 150 psalms in the Book of Psalms, and he perhaps wrote others where no author is identified. When one reads the psalms that were written by King David, it's easy to see how much he loved and trusted God, and yes, how he even obeyed God usually. He also was quick to repent of his sins once he was confronted, so King David became God's gold standard for future human, earthly kings. With all of King David's failures, he was still greatly loved by God. We see men so differently than God sees them. David was a mere shepherd boy when he was chosen by God to be king. God gave David the strength and skill to kill a bear, a lion, and a giant because he honored the Lord, but he often was weak morally.

Democrats, establishment Republicans, RINOs, and most Christians today would totally reject King David as a political leader, and most women would dismiss him as a potential husband. He wouldn't be a man after most human hearts. God truly sees people differently because He can see the motives of the heart.

After the reign of King David, his son Solomon became the next king of Israel. Solomon began well, and he asked God to give him an understanding heart, able to discern good and evil, rather than asking for great riches. Because of his request, God blessed Solomon with great wisdom and great wealth. King Solomon ruled Israel with such godly wisdom that queens and kings from surrounding nations were astounded by his knowledge. Solomon was the principal author of the Book of Proverbs—a book that is absolutely loaded with wisdom. Solomon also wrote the Book of Ecclesiastes and the Song of Solomon (Song of Songs). His writings are beautiful and full of wisdom; the seven pillars of wisdom are found in the writings of Solomon in the Book of Proverbs. But King Solomon had one gigantic problem: He loved foreign women—and lots of them! Solomon married seven hundred wives and had three hundred concubines—a total of one thousand women! King Solomon's foreign wives were idol worshipers and they served false gods. They eventually turned Solomon's heart away from the Lord God of Israel, and he too, became a worshiper of false deities. King Solomon had great wisdom, but in the end, he used it foolishly.

Solomon also was a harsh ruler, but initially he loved God and remained devoted to Him until his idol-worshiping wives turned his heart away from the Lord. He spent seven years building a beautiful temple for the Lord, but he spent thirteen years building a grand palace for himself. Perhaps he needed a palace of that scale to accommodate (and separate) all those wives! For David's sake, the Lord remained faithful to King Solomon, even though Solomon didn't remain loyal to Him. God also showed Solomon tremendous grace by not allowing the kingdom of Israel to be divided while he was still king; it was split after Solomon's reign.

When Solomon's reign ended, his son Rehoboam became king over Israel. King Rehoboam was a harsh ruler and an evil man, and the people rebelled against him. He had less of an appetite for women than his father, King Solomon, had; he had only eighteen wives and sixty concubines. The Lord was very good to King Rehoboam, but Rehoboam turned away from serving God anyway. The Lord allowed the king of Egypt to attack Jerusalem, but He didn't allow King Rehoboam or the people to be destroyed completely. God protected them from total annihilation. The Lord did, however, allow Israel to be divided into a northern kingdom and southern kingdom. The northern kingdom, known as Israel, included ten of the twelve tribes of Jacob. The southern kingdom of Judah consisted of only two tribes, Judah and Benjamin. For King David's sake, God allowed kings from the tribe of Judah to continue to sit on the throne of David. Jesus Christ, the perfect King of the Jews, through His earthly lineage was also from the tribe of Judah.

It's interesting to note that after the kingdom was split, no good kings ruled the northern kingdom of Israel. The southern kingdom of Judah did slightly better; it had eight good kings. But based on their actions, it's difficult to easily ascertain who the good kings were and who the bad kings were. The distinguishing factor seems to have been whether or not the kings loved God and encouraged the people to serve God and obey His commands. I believe this same application can be used today to distinguish a good president or world leader from a bad leader. This is not to say that leaders claiming to be Christians can necessarily be trusted to be actual followers of Christ. Just because someone quotes a Bible scripture or teaches a Sunday school class doesn't automatically mean they love the Lord and promote Christian values. A leader's political ideology must also be considered to determine if they'll comply with God's will for the nation. A leader just being a Christian isn't enough; some Christians are foolish and rule in an ungodly manner. To be a good king or leader, a politician must be a promoter of Christian values and wise by God's standards.

Godly wisdom, along with a steadfast commitment to God's will, is the defining trait of a good leader. Knowledge or wisdom without adherence to God's will is useless, and it causes a leader and a country to end up in a ditch. No leader serves the Lord perfectly, but this shouldn't stop them from trying to execute the will of God as frequently as possible. It might be a good idea and a valuable lesson for modern-day leaders to study the accounts of the various kings in the Old Testament to amass information about successful, as well as unsuccessful leadership. This could help leaders avoid pitfalls and give them an advantage in dealing with difficult issues. Every good leader needs God's guidance and needs to surround himself or herself with godly people and wise counselors. Many times, leaders are only as good as those they choose to surround themselves with. This is as true today as it was in biblical times.

For example, some presidential administrations have relied on poor advisors, and in some instances unqualified counselors, to guide them in making important decisions. The result has been unacceptable trade deals, costly wars, breached national security, undesirable health care legislation, and a host of other poor legislative decisions. Good advisors and wise counselors are of paramount importance for kings and presidents to be successful leaders. In biblical times, advisors were equally important. The good kings listened to good advisors and surrounded themselves with godly counselors. Bad or evil kings were foolish, and they didn't heed sound advice.

King Rehoboam is a perfect example of this in the Old Testament. When he became king, he was asked to reduce the heavy burdens levied on the people of Israel by King Solomon's administration. King Rehoboam first consulted the elders who had formerly worked for his father, Solomon, and they advised him to be kinder and gentler to the people. He rejected their good advice and instead sought the advice of more youthful counselors with whom he had grown up. They advised him to be even harsher to the people, and this was the advice he accepted and implemented. So, it should come as no surprise that the people revolted. The final result of King Rehoboam's harsh leadership was that the kingdom of Israel was divided into two parts. The lineage of King David continued to rule the southern kingdom of Judah until they were taken into captivity.

It's interesting to note that King David reigned as king for forty years, and his son Solomon also reigned for forty years. David reigned seven years in Judah and thirty-three years over all of the tribes of Israel. But with Rehoboam, the kingdom was divided, and due to ungodly leadership, ancient Israel was captured and eventually destroyed by the Assyrians. The tribes were dispersed; today they are often referred to as the "ten lost tribes of Israel." The kingdom of Judah outlasted the kingdom of Israel, but it eventually was also captured by Babylon and remained in captivity for seventy years. God allowed King Nebuchadnezzar of Babylon to take Judah captive, and He used him to bring correction to the people of Judah. Throughout the Old Testament, God routinely used pagan kings or nations to discipline His children, but He often also used them to be a blessing to His people. Discipline or blessing was meted out based upon the unfaithfulness or faithfulness of the children of God. This theme runs throughout the Scriptures, and we are all advised to choose faithfulness and blessing.

Another interesting theme in the Old Testament is that evil and destruction could come upon a nation for the sins of its previous corrupt leaders. Should the United States of America be concerned? Some people believe the September 11th terrorist attacks happened as a result of the sins of our previous leaders, and others think the invasion of our country by illegal immigrants and the drug epidemic are a result of the same. Some people believe the depravity of so many individuals is the judgment of God today in the form of turning people over to their reprobate minds for rejecting the Lord. A nation that doesn't honor God, especially its top leaders, is a nation in serious trouble. This has been proven true both from history and from the Scriptures. When ungodly people rule, evil will prevail in a nation; although the Lord is patient, He eventually punishes evil.

This certainly was a belief postulated in biblical times. The kingdom of Israel had zero good kings, it had loads of problems, and it was eventually destroyed by enemies that God allowed to chastise the people for their ungodliness. The kingdom of Judah had many evil kings, it had a few good kings, and it also was eventually overthrown by its enemies, whom God sent to punish the people for their sins and unfaithfulness. There were some decent, godly people within the ranks of the Israelites, but when the kingdom was punished, everybody suffered. The godly suffered along with the ungodly. The entire nation prospered or suffered based on the godly attributes or lack thereof by the kingly leadership.

The first king of the northern kingdom after the split was Jeroboam. Fear and insecurity contributed to his downfall. King Jeroboam wouldn't allow the people to go to Jerusalem to worship God, because he feared they might desert him and join the southern kingdom of Judah. He foolishly made false gods for the people to worship. Some of the Levites did depart from Israel—they probably didn't want to worship false gods—and relocated to the land of Judah. A number of kings ruled the northern kingdom over the next two hundred years or so before they were captured by the Assyrians. Two of the most notorious and worst kings ruling over Israel were Omri and Ahab.

The southern kingdom of Judah had a mixture of good and bad kings. Perhaps one of the most infamous kings of Judah was Manasseh. He was Hezekiah's son. Interestingly, Manasseh was born to Hezekiah and his wife after Hezekiah had a serious illness and was going to die. King Hezekiah prayed and begged the Lord to spare his life, and the Lord granted his request— adding fifteen more years to his life. During this period, his son Manasseh was born. This is stunning to me—since God knows everything. He knew the additional years given to Hezekiah would later result in a very evil king being added to his lineage in Judah. There were a number of evil kings who reigned over Judah, but Manasseh was extremely wicked. The good kings were Asa, Jehoshaphat, Joash, Amaziah, Uzziah (also known as Azariah), Jotham, Hezekiah, and Josiah.

Some of the good kings of Judah were not exactly stellar characters, and they didn't worship the Lord wholeheartedly. Most of these kings failed to drain the swamp, so to speak! For example, Kings Asa and Jehoshaphat did right in the sight of the Lord by removing false idols, but they didn't remove the high places (the pagan places of worship) in Judah. King Joash was a good king who did right in the sight of the Lord—until the priest Jehoiada died (see 2 Kings 12; 2 Chronicles 24). Then Joash forsook the Lord and also killed Jehoiada's son Zechariah for prophesying that he should clean up his act. Later King Joash's own men killed him after he was wounded by the Syrian army.

The Bible records that Amaziah was a good king who did right in the sight of the Lord, but he did not do it with a loyal heart! He executed the men who were responsible for killing his father, King Joash. He also later turned his heart away from the Lord and worshiped idols. Some of his servants also killed him—like father, like son!

King Azariah, also known as Uzziah, did right in the sight of the Lord and sought God, as long as the priest was mentoring him. He became strong and famous, and then he sinned against the Lord. God struck him with leprosy until the day of his death.

King Jotham was a good king who served the Lord all the days of his life even though the people of Judah acted corruptly. King Hezekiah was a good king who loved and served God. He also encouraged the priests and other people to praise and worship the Lord. God gave King Hezekiah great riches and honor. But when he became prideful, the Lord disciplined him. King Hezekiah was one of the few kings to remain faithful to God.

King Josiah was a good king, who removed the high places, destroyed idols, and tore down the altars of Baal. He was grieved to recognize how his forefathers had failed God after the Book of the Law was found and read to him. King Josiah also kept the Passover. But he made one mistake that cost him his life—he went to war with Egypt without consulting God. He went to war with a nation with whom the Lord had never intended him to go to war. Sound familiar?

So that was a recap of the good kings of Judah. Just strictly observing their lives and behavior, it would be nearly impossible to identify several of them as good kings. The good kings served the Lord, some of them halfheartedly, but most of them didn't remove the high places or the pagan places of worship entirely. Most of the good kings were barely distinguishable from the bad kings. The best kings among the good kings were buried with distinction and honor, while other kings weren't buried with the more honorable kings.

So, what are some of the takeaways or major lessons we learn from studying the biblical accounts of Israel's leaders and kings? The greatest lesson from Judge Samuel, King David, and most of the other kings of Israel: *Train and discipline your children well.* Proverbs 22:6 says, "Train up a child in the way he should go, and when he is old he will not depart from it." And Proverbs 10:1 states, "A wise son makes a glad father, but a foolish son is the grief of his mother." How many of us have seen mothers standing in courtrooms or at gravesites grieving over sons who foolishly went astray? And, I might add, foolish individuals who grow up to become leaders not only grieve their parents, but they also grieve those whom they govern. Proverbs 13:24 says, "He who spares his rod hates his son, but he who loves him disciplines him promptly." This is not suggesting that parents beat their children, but rather that wise parents are to properly teach and discipline their children; how else will youth learn right from wrong or safe from harmful? Further, Proverbs 29:15 states, "The rod and rebuke give wisdom, but a child left to himself brings shame to his mother." Again, parents are admonished to discipline their children, so they will gain wisdom and become productive members of society. Interestingly, these proverbs—inspired by God—were written by King Solomon, who seemingly neither listened to God's guidance nor took his own advice.

An important lesson from King Saul: *Remain humble, and stay small in your own eyes.* The Bible says in James 4:6, "God resists the proud, but gives grace to the humble." And Proverbs 16:18b states, "Pride goes before destruction, and a haughty spirit before a fall." Other lessons from King Saul's life are: *Don't be overcome by the green-eyed monster of jealousy, because it might eventually destroy you, and it might even destroy members of your family in the process. Remain obedient to God and accept His will. It's not how you start, but how you finish.* The Bible indicates that jealousy is as cruel as the grave (Song of Solomon 8:6). Throughout the Word of God, we're instructed to be obedient to the Lord and fulfill His will for our lives—not our will, but His will be done. We're also directed to run a good race, to stay on course and remain true to our faith, and to finish the race well. King Saul did none of these things.

Important lessons from King David: *Love God with all of your heart, and He will help you slay all the bears, lions, and giants in your spiritual life.* Mark 12:30–31 says, "You shall love the Lord your God with all your heart, with all your soul, with all your mind, and with all your strength. This is the first commandment. And the second, like it, is this: You shall love your neighbor as yourself. There is no other commandment greater than these." If we could do this successfully, we would spare ourselves a lot of trouble. Other lessons from King David's life include: *Don't covet your neighbor's wife, nor commit adultery with her. Don't have multiple wives. Love and respect your wife, and don't treat a wife as a piece of property. Don't take another man's wife, even one that formerly belonged to you* (Exodus 20:14, 17; Deuteronomy 5:18, 21; Matthew 19:6; Ephesians 5:25). *Do not commit murder* (Exodus 20:13; Deuteronomy 5:17). *Accept God's punishment and be quick to repent.* Proverbs 3:11–12 says, "Do not despise the chastening of the LORD, nor detest His correction. For whom the LORD loves He corrects, just as a father the son in whom he delights." Proverbs 12:1 further states that anyone who hates correction is stupid. We also learn from King David's life to train children to have godly love and respect for each other, and to train them to respect their parents and not be in competition with each other. Proverbs 20:20 says, "Whoever curses his father or his mother, his lamp will be put out in deep darkness." Also, the Ten Commandments in Exodus 20:12 and Deuteronomy 5:16 direct us to honor our fathers and mothers. And Ephesians 6:2, likewise, instructs us to honor our parents, and indicates that this is the first commandment with a promise. Ephesians 6:3 states the promise as, "That it may be well with you and you may live long on the earth." Another lesson we can learn from King David's life is to remain loyal to your friends and be a blessing to their children: this he excelled at. The Bible indicates that for us to have friends, we must first show ourselves to be friendly to others (Proverbs 18:24). Yet another lesson we learn is not to take matters into our own hands when we're persecuted and treated unfairly, but to wait on the Lord to deliver us. Proverbs 3:5 tells us to trust in the Lord with all of our hearts. Also, Proverbs 20:22 states, "Do not say, 'I will repay evil'; wait for the LORD, and He will save you" (NASB). And one of the most amazing lessons that we can learn from King

David's life is that you don't have to be perfect—or even nearly perfect—for God to love you and to show you abundant favor!

Lessons from King Solomon and his son Rehoboam include the following: *One wife is enough, or at least one wife at a time is sufficient. Marry a godly woman who loves the Lord.* Proverbs 31:30 says, "Charm is deceitful and beauty is passing, but a woman who fears the LORD—she shall be praised." Other lessons from the lives of King Solomon and his son are to make wisdom the principle thing in one's life and to choose friends carefully. Also, treat those you govern with respect (do not call them "deplorable," and don't levy heavy taxes on them)! Proverbs 4:7 states, "Wisdom is the principal thing; therefore, get wisdom. And in all your getting, get understanding." Proverbs 12:15 says, "The way of a fool is right in his own eyes, but he who heeds counsel is wise." I might add that for an individual to be wise and be able to make appropriate decisions, he or she must heed—not just counsel—but wise counsel. Proverbs 1:5 states, "A wise man will hear and increase learning, and a man of understanding will attain wise counsel." And Proverbs 13:20 tells us, "He who walks with wise men will be wise, but the companion of fools will be destroyed." If foolish and ungodly people aren't destroyed in this life, they most certainly will be destroyed in the next. No one will escape final punishment—or final reward—from God.

One of the major lessons men can learn from King Ahab's life is this: *Marry wisely.* This he did not do. The Bible says in Proverbs 12:4, "An excellent wife is the crown of her husband, but she who causes shame is like rottenness in his bones." A lesson we learn from the reign of King Josiah is this: *Do not go to war without first consulting the Lord.* A few other lessons from the history of the kings of Israel include to fear (reverence) God and not to fear man. Also, it's important for leaders to follow the advice of *godly* spiritual mentors. Another important lesson is to trust in the power of God, and not in the strength of man or in military might. Jeremiah 17:7 says, "Blessed is the man who trusts in the LORD, whose confidence is in Him" (NIV). Jeremiah 17:5 tells us that anyone who trusts in man rather than God is cursed, so it's very important who we put our trust in. A lesson none of us should ever forget is that there are consequences for being unfaithful to God. Again, it's not how one starts, but it's very important how one finishes. It's also of the utmost importance to ask for God's advice when choosing our leaders, especially today, when we have the privilege of electing our leaders! But the most important lesson of all is to know and follow the one perfect King! First Chronicles 16:11 says, "Seek the LORD and his strength; seek his face continually" (KJV).

There are probably many other lessons we can learn from the history of the numerous kings of Israel, if people care to read the accounts and dig them out for themselves. I've only mentioned a few lessons the Lord revealed to me. After studying the history of the kings of Israel and Judah, I'm happy I live in this day and age and in the United States of America—where Donald J. Trump is the president. I would take President Trump over any of the kings of ancient Israel! But I do encourage people to study the history of Israel and Judah to avoid the mistakes they made in serving the Lord.

I also encourage people to look at President Trump and other world leaders as God sees them, not through their own natural eyes. Again, a good leader promotes Christian values and religious freedom, makes wise decisions concerning legislation, uses wisdom in foreign affairs (especially dealing with the state of Israel and our closest allies), and encourages people to honor God. A good leader also must be patriotic and love his country and its citizens. Look closely, and you will be able to identify these traits in President Trump. Our president is clearly a "good king," but the only "perfect King" is the Lord Jesus Christ!

It's foolish and unproductive for people to seek a perfect president or a flawless world leader, for none exists; the search is futile. There's only one perfect Ruler—the Lord Jesus Christ! So undoubtedly, we can expect some mediocre leaders, fewer good leaders, and perhaps many bad leaders to preside over the United States. By making wiser political choices, however, we can minimize the number of undesirable leaders we have and mitigate the damaging results of their poor leadership.

When viewing history, people are divided about the merits or shortcomings of our U.S. presidents. Among presidential historians, Abraham Lincoln consistently ranks as our best president ever, although he wasn't always so honored or revered by Democrats due to his antislavery stance. But he is now viewed by both Democrats and Republicans alike as a great American hero. Historians usually rank George Washington and Franklin Delano Roosevelt as the top two and three best presidents—sometimes the order is reversed. Not everyone agrees with these rankings. I think most people would agree that President Abraham Lincoln was a great man and perhaps our best president. He gave his very life in the pursuit of abolishing slavery to ensure that all men and women in the United States truly had equal rights. Many people might concur that George Washington earned the title of good president and national hero, but there is the issue of slave ownership so common in our early history; George Washington certainly owned slaves. In addition, some Republicans and Democrats would agree with the ranking of FDR, while others would vehemently disagree.

Presidential historians and political science scholars might not agree with me, but I would rank President Ronald Reagan and President Donald J. Trump as two of our best presidents in recent times, and three of our worst presidents as Jimmy Carter, Bill Clinton, and Barack Obama. I have based my assessment on how these presidents handled foreign affairs—particularly relating to the Middle East and Israel—the economy, both legal and illegal immigration, the armed forces, religious liberty, and also how they treated White House staff, secret service agents, and other individuals serving them. (Trust me, word gets around in D.C. how White House staff are treated by the First Families.)

President Trump exhibits strong and decisive leadership in handling foreign affairs and important matters here at home. He treats staff members with dignity and respect; even voters are treated as valued members of his team. This makes him highly esteemed among loyal supporters, but dissenters and adversaries continue to remain hostile and confrontational toward him and his administration. They resist the rebuilding of our fractured foundations, but to resist that which is beneficial to them and good for the country doesn't demonstrate soundness of mind. In fact, it's the personification of stupidity.

CHAPTER 10

The Epitome of Stupidity

There is a way that seems right to a man,
but its end is the way of death.
PROVERBS 14:12 NKJV

Resisting what is beneficial for the United States and its citizens, and then advocating what is detrimental to our country, is the absolute epitome of stupidity. Also, professing liberal political ideology as one's theology, and substituting it for the doctrine of Christ, is unwise. Choosing the former is sure to desolate one's country, and the latter is certain to doom one's soul. Some individuals claim that liberal political ideology is equivalent to and even indistinguishable from the theology of Christ, but this is absolutely absurd. It's foolish for individuals to claim that liberalism and Christianity are somehow compatible. *They aren't, nor will they ever be!* They're diametrically opposed to one another.

This kind of paganism has existed throughout history, but it has never been more on display in America than it is today. Our nation has a great Christian heritage, but as the culture has grown more secular, many people no longer express a belief in Christ. Sadly, we've become a post-Christian society, it seems, almost overnight. Many individuals—especially millennials—accept non-Christian doctrine, to include various false religions, the occult, atheism, paganism, and New Age. Many people in the political arena like to substitute liberalism for the Gospel of Christ, which surprisingly has even been accepted by members of some supposedly Christian churches.

Unfortunately, Christians have been guilty of abdicating the throne of righteousness to secular politics and relinquishing institutions to ungodliness that once were dedicated to Christ. We foolishly allow atheists to dictate what our country stands for or against, by electing ungodly politicians who appoint liberal judges that legislate from the bench. In the past, we gave the courts the authority to misinterpret law, separating church and state. Now activist judges in lower district courts wield enormous power clearly never intended by our Constitution. The U.S. Constitution established three distinct branches of government precisely to prevent this type of abuse of power. Yet most of us have stood silently by and allowed liberal courts to dictate ungodly policy. In hindsight, we can see how remaining silent when we should have spoken up was the epitome of stupidity.

Why did we not stand more firmly against atheism and secular politics, and boldly proclaim the Gospel of Christ? How did we surrender so much territory so easily and so quickly to those who deny our Christian heritage and the existence of Jesus Christ? Before the great capitulation on the part of the United States Supreme Court to liberal thought, and the rise of destructive atheists like Madalyn Murray O'Hair, kids grew up in a culture that allowed prayer and Bible reading in schools and biblical beliefs to be taught in classrooms. Then, suddenly, Baby Boomers and Generation X fell victim to radical communist ideology and atheistic politics almost overnight. And still continuing today, millennials (Generation Y), Generation Z, and beyond can no longer learn God's standards in public schools or secular places of higher learning; unfortunately, most of them also don't learn them at home either. Nowadays, youth are much more likely to hear about the Big Bang Theory than they are to hear about God's creation story. Things weren't like that when I was growing up.

Both schools and science promote the concept of the big bang, but to believe this theory and deny creationism is sheer foolishness. I agree with scientists that there was a big bang, but it was not as they believe. The big bang happened when Lucifer rebelled against God and was tossed out of heaven! That's the only "big bang" in which people should believe, because it's the only one that actually happened. However, the Big Bang Theory is still routinely accepted by some scientists and other gullible individuals as fact—the absolute epitome of stupidity.

I don't recall being taught the Big Bang Theory when I went to school, but I've heard a lot about it ever since. Being a Christian, naturally, I don't adhere to the Big Bang Theory of creation. But a few years ago, I came in contact with the theory while visiting a planetarium in New York City. While waiting in the lobby of the theater, we heard a short presentation of the origin of the universe—which they described as the big bang! I was very disappointed, and I stood there quietly debunking the myth in my mind. The planetarium's main presentation, likewise, was a great disappointment—a total waste of money. It could've been exciting if they had shown a giant explosion with Lucifer falling from the heavens. Now that would have been something worth seeing! Recently, I visited the Museum of Natural History in Albuquerque, New Mexico; I don't recall hearing anything about the big bang. But the show at the planetarium was tediously boring. It could have been interesting if it had included the origin of the planets—with some scriptures about God's greatness flashed across the screen. Imagine a show with God creating the heavens and the earth as indicated in Genesis 1, and displaying scriptures across the screen with God's voice saying, "Let there be!" Also, imagine displaying **Psalm 74:16–17, which states, "The day is Yours; the night also is Yours; You have prepared the light and the sun. You have set all the borders of the earth; You have made summer and winter,"** followed by scenes from the earth—day dawning, sunshine, and the brilliance of a day and activity on earth. A scene of night on earth could show a beautiful city with all its lovely nighttime lights. Other scenes could show the beauty of summer on earth, and the beautiful contrast of winter—while at the same time showing scenes from other planets. Imagine also God counting the stars and calling them all by name, as indicated in Psalm 147:4. Just imagine God's booming voice calling out the names of stars—some names we know and others we've never heard before—and a string of numbers stretching across the screen and disappearing off the screen, because the number of stars is limitless. Only God knows the number of stars in heaven; it is too many for human beings to count—plus the universe and the stars are constantly increasing. And rather than a big bang explanation, the show could incorporate the war in heaven with Lucifer—*pow, pow, pow, bang,* and a massive explosion. Then Lucifer could be shown as a beautiful angel falling from heaven and turning into a grotesque creature before striking earth—with total chaos when he hits the earth. Now that would be a planetarium show worth watching—and worth paying for!

The display at the Albuquerque Museum about the human brain also failed to impress me because of its strictly secular perspective. The brain display would have been much more interesting if the museum had included information about how to renew one's mind with the Word of God. Also, it would have been great to see a presentation conducted by brain expert and cognitive neuroscientist Dr. Caroline Leaf—showing how one can actually change the brain, improve mental health, and get rid of toxic thoughts simply by diet and renewing one's mind.

The possibilities are infinite when God is allowed to be involved in our lives—even in museum presentations—but I realize most museums are partially government-funded, and this has hamstrung them in what they can do. God and the story of divine creation are prohibited from public government-funded museums—the result of that nasty court decision demanding the separation of church and state based on a misinterpretation of the Establishment Clause in the First Amendment! The Lord has been essentially eliminated from public life in the United States, even in many churches, because the Lord of all creation has become offensive to many Americans.

God was initially honored in our country, and prayer was allowed to be offered to Him in public schools. Until 1962, even in New York State schools, prayer to almighty God was recited every morning. The prayer that was sanctioned by the board of education was sweet and seemingly unthreatening, but a few Jewish families, along with a couple of other liberals, found it offensive. The prayer simply stated, "Almighty God, we acknowledge our dependence upon Thee, and we beg Thy blessings upon us, our parents, our teachers, and our country. Amen."[9] So, how could this prayer possibly offend anyone? It doesn't even mention the name of Jesus! But somehow it offended liberals, and a lawsuit was brought against the school board president (*Engel v. Vitale*)—and the United States Supreme Court decided in favor of Mr. Steven Engel and the other dissenters who joined him. The school board president, Mr. William Vitale Jr., was slapped with the charge of violating the Establishment Clause of the First Amendment of the United States Constitution. Then in 1963, Madalyn Murray (who became Madalyn Murray O'Hair in 1965) likewise won her case, citing Bible reading in public schools as unconstitutional. Atheists, with the help of liberal justices, perhaps have forever removed sanctioned prayer from our public schools, and God and the Bible were relegated to the basement! This is the epitome of stupidity.

These defeats for Christianity were big wins for liberalism, atheism, and communism in the early 1960s. This decade was a period in our history overwhelmed with contrasting points of view, as is true in almost every decade. We experienced a time of peace and a time of war, a time of civility, love, innocence, peaceful civil rights protests, and patriotism, but also a time of incivility, hatred, racism, radical antiwar protests, atheism, and rebellion! The 1960s was a time of wide-eyed innocence and at the same time blatant immorality, a time when conservative values were honored, but also a time of opposition to traditional values, turmoil, and deep spiritual darkness. Our way forward as a nation was forever changed by the sexual revolution, and the two radical U.S. Supreme Court decisions misinterpreting the Establishment Clause that gave way to secularism and a favored status for atheism over Christianity. Also, our history was forever marred in the 1960s by the horrific assassinations of three of our most prominent citizens at that time—President John F. Kennedy, Dr. Martin Luther King Jr., and Robert F. Kennedy. This was diabolical and horrific stupidity.

Then came the 1970s, with continued antiwar protests and another radical Supreme Court decision—a decision that would forever change the moral landscape and the face of politics in the United States. *Roe v. Wade* was a distinct demarcation as well as a dark landmark decision by the Supreme Court to legalize abortion. Due to these radical Supreme Court decisions, both atheism and murder are now sanctioned by the courts.

Madalyn Murray O'Hair continued to be the ugly face of atheism in the United States in the 1970s and onward, to the day of her death. Incidentally, Madalyn O'Hair supported Jimmy Carter for president in 1976, because of his stance on separation of church and state, his opposition to mandatory school prayer, and his support for sex education in public schools. If atheists had been unsuccessful in defeating prayer and Bible reading in public schools in the 1960s, they surely would have gained a sympathetic ear and success under the Carter administration. Admittedly, President Carter has always been a bit of an enigma to me. He taught Sunday school classes at his Baptist church for a number of years, and he has worked in cooperation with Habitat for Humanity building affordable housing for the poor, yet many of his views do not line up with those in the Scriptures. Although Carter doesn't believe in abortion personally, he believes abortion should be legal. His personal opinion is that Jesus would approve of same-sex marriage, but he's unable to point to a single scripture in the Bible to support this belief. It's surprising that a man who claims to be a born-again believer and has taught the Bible for numerous years is uncertain what the Scriptures say about various issues. Evidently, Carter also believes Israel is a big bully, and that the Palestinians are just poor, misunderstood victims. Some people view President Carter as anti-Semitic, while others believe his political and personal perspectives are based on monetary gain from the Arabs. Again, Carter's views are puzzling—I don't understand his mindset.

At any rate, it seems that every decade produces paradoxes, enigmas, antithetical views, and vastly contrasting political ideologies. Our nation truly is a tale of two cities, as is every other nation on the planet, because we exist in a fallen world with two kingdoms in operation. This is how Christianity and atheism can exist at the same time, and why both conservative and liberal theology can be so prevalent during the same time period. But for intelligent people to accept radical ideologies and still vote for radical politicians is the epitome of stupidity.

The Kingdom of Light and the Kingdom of Darkness coexist in every era, and they work simultaneously in every age in direct opposition to one another. Atheism had been around for a long time, but it experienced a surge in the United States in the 1960s and a resurgence called the New Atheism Movement in the early 2000s. This new movement consists of several outspoken critics of faith, Christianity in particular, who have a vendetta against God. Both left-leaning unelected officials (the courts) and liberal elected politicians in the United States continue to remain sympathetic toward atheists. For example, in 2015, Madison, Wisconsin, became the first city in America to pass an ordinance granting equal rights to atheists. Then in 2016, President Obama signed a law extending protection to non-theists and people claiming no religion in particular. Also, liberal courts have continued to side with ungodly individuals, in many cases against Christians. All of these unsound actions are the epitome of stupidity.

Courts in particular have been vocal advocates of atheism. Liberal courts in the United States have interfered so drastically and in such a negative way in our lives that now the primary ways for people to hear about God is in the privacy of their own homes, from courageous street preachers, from privately owned and funded museums—like the Ark Encounter in Kentucky, the Billy Graham Library located in North Carolina, and the Museum of the Bible in Washington, D.C., and, of course, churches. But unbelievers aren't exactly flocking to churches these days, nor are all pastors bold enough to preach the full Gospel of Jesus Christ.

I'm grateful I spent my early formative years in an age when prayer was allowed in school, when the Gospel was proclaimed freely, and when politics were fairly conservative in the United States of America. I'm also happy that I eventually became a Christian and a political conservative, for rejecting Christ and opposing conservative politics is profoundly stupid. The first is sure to damn one's eternal soul, while the other is sure to damage one's earthly existence.

Being inactive politically or voting for radicals that are sure to doom one's life is totally illogical, and the epitome of stupidity! Some people who support ungodly policies consider themselves liberal Christians, but how can anyone reconcile the Christian faith with liberalism? The term "liberal Christian" is a misnomer, because the terms "liberal" and "Christian" are incompatible and simply can't be harmonized. Christian faith, the Word of God, and liberalism cannot be integrated.

An individual who adamantly claims to be a Christian recently told me that she is a Democrat and votes for Democrats even though she doesn't agree with their ideology. She also told me she plans to stop reading the Bible, because it conflicts with her politics! She thinks the Word of God is controversial and potentially very offensive to unbelievers, so sharing the Gospel is unwise and should be curtailed. Her commitment to politics clearly far outweighs her commitment to Jesus Christ. To say I was stunned by her admission would be an understatement; I was absolutely flabbergasted. After this particular conversation, I realized this individual most likely had never experienced a genuine born-again conversion to Christ.

To vote for a political party whose views you oppose is the epitome of stupidity! But there are thousands of voters with this mindset; they totally disagree with the Democrat Party platform and they may even be offended by many of the candidates, but they vote for them anyway. Some of these individuals were born Democrats and will die Democrats!

People often have the same mindset concerning religion. I once took a Catholic friend to a nondenominational church with me, and she loved it. She commented about how boring her Catholic services were and how she got nothing at all out of the homily—but she continued to remain very loyal. I suggested the Lord might be leading her to switch loyalties. She exclaimed, "Goodness, no, I can't leave the Catholic Church. I was born a Catholic, and I'll die a Catholic!" But the Bible tells us that in order to enter the kingdom of heaven, our righteousness must exceed that of the scribes and Pharisees (see Matthew 5:20). The scribes and Pharisees had religion, went to the synagogue every day, prayed and fasted often, kept the rules, but they didn't know God. It seems to me that an awful lot of people have steadfast loyalty to their religion and pledge undying allegiance to their political party, but they know not to whom or to what they're paying homage. They need to become *woke* to Jesus Christ.

Thankfully, some individuals do wake up eventually, but it sometimes takes a major event for them to wake up—such as the election of radical candidates. A conservative county clerk in Morehead, Kentucky, woke up during the second term of President Obama. Evidently, the county clerk had been a Democrat all of her life—and she had presumably voted Democrat as well. During the second term of the Obama administration and with the enactment of same-sex marriage laws, she suddenly decided as a Christian and in good conscience that she couldn't issue same-sex marriage licenses. She was jailed for refusing to sign off on marriage applications for same-sex couples, and her civil disobedience made headline news. I think she had a right to object to a law with which she disagreed, but I don't necessarily believe she had a right to object to this particular law. The reason for my belief is that she was a Democrat, and she had presumably voted for Obama twice, and then she voiced an objection against a piece of legislation that, in essence, she herself had helped to pass. This is the epitome of stupidity! Now, if I'm wrong about the county clerk and she didn't vote for President Obama, then I owe her an apology. I'm glad that, like other slumbering Democrats, she finally woke up and decided to join the Republican Party. No born-again believer in Christ should be a member of a radical political party. This is the very essence of stupidity!

Radicals convincing citizens that our government should be eliminated and replaced by a socialist form of government, likewise, is absurd, the epitome of stupidity! Other actions Democrats take that also rise to the level of the epitome of stupidity include trying to convict innocent people of crimes they themselves are guilty of, apologizing for being white, calling black conservatives white supremacists, trying to change their ethnicity or race, and trying to convince folks that dirty old men are simply demonstrative, friendly people—yeah, right! A man invading a woman's space and constantly touching women is not exhibiting fondness or being friendly—he's hoping to grab a hand full of something! I've lived on this earth almost seven decades, and I've walked around the block more than once! I'm not buying that lie any time in this century!

There is a whole myriad of other nonsensical concepts and outrageous antics that dishonest politicians have invented to cover their misdeeds and advance their extremist agenda, and then force undesirable legislation upon us. Any good, sound government legislation is debated and fought against for years before being passed—if it gets passed at all. The political environment is so toxic in Washington, D.C. that nothing gets done in an efficient, cost-effective manner. Our national debt is soaring, but liberal politicians continue to spend unnecessary funds debating, debating, debating, opposing, and investigating continuously. This is the epitome of stupidity! While the country drowns in debt, they also take long, expensive trips at the taxpayers' expense, and when they are on Capitol Hill, they oppose, debate, and investigate everything to death—they can't act any dumber than this!

Some politicians appear to oppose good legislation just to be contrary. This clearly was displayed by the failure to repeal Obamacare. The repeal of Obamacare didn't fail because it was a bad idea for the people, but rather because of political toxicity and nasty personality disorders! This piece of legislation had the fingerprints of the devil all over it from the very start—when it initially passed Congress and when it failed to be repealed. An untold number of U.S. citizens have been injured financially by this ill-conceived health care law, including several members of my family. Obamacare was just another source of contention and division perpetrated by godless people, but it was sold to the American public as a wonderful concept of great benefit. Both political parties knew from the outset that it was a bad idea, but radical Democrats forced this unpopular piece of legislation upon the citizens anyway. Obnoxious politicians pursued this legislation for their own self-interest and to pacify fragile egos while constituents suffered the consequences. This is wrong and just plain dumb, and to continue to put them in office and embrace their radical ideology is the epitome of stupidity!

Radicals always ruin what they touch, and they have a tarnished history of defecating all over conservative cities and states, and then leaving them in disarray. Once they've ruined formerly conservative areas of the country and can't stand the foul stench any longer, they pick up their things and move on to other conservative areas and begin the defecation process all over again. Radicals never learn from history or failure. It's always somebody else's fault! According to them, President Reagan was to blame, President Trump is responsible, or perhaps further back in history, President Lincoln was the guilty party! But it's never, ever them. These folks just keep defecating everywhere, and once an area is ravaged, then sometimes a conservative is called in to fix things—but things usually can't be fixed. Once Venezuela is destroyed, it's pretty difficult to restore it to its former prosperous self. The radicals never learn, and they never make the connection to themselves, so the defecating process never ceases, and it becomes an endless cycle. This is the epitome of stupidity!

According to the radicals, climate change will kill the entire planet within the next ten to twelve years. Radicals are seriously alarmed about this issue; yet they seem unaware of the danger they themselves pose to our country and the planet. Climate change is not the problem; radical ideology, if not stopped, is what will eventually destroy us! People need to wake up and escape the liberal lunacy while there's still a chance to escape. Supporting radical candidates and their reckless policies is absolutely the epitome of stupidity!

Listening to liberal "fake news" outlets, likewise, is unwise. It's rumored that the FOX News Network is considering making its programming less conservative, and if this is true, it reflects boundless stupidity. Also, suspending conservative hosts for perceived infractions of nonexistent rules of journalism shows contempt for FOX network viewers. Only conservatives watch

FOX on a regular basis, so program changes promoting a liberal agenda or radical ideology would be truly asinine and the epitome of stupidity! My husband and I, like many other viewers, have become increasingly disappointed with FOX Network programming. We sincerely hope FOX executives receive a wakeup call soon. (We don't watch Trump haters; we won't watch Chris Wallace, Judge Napolitano, or several other liberals, and we never watched Shepard Smith.)

The GOP also needs a wakeup call to ensure that viable candidates are encouraged to run for office. Conservative voters don't want to have to choose between liberal RINOs and Democrats. We escaped a bullet in 2016! RINOs cannot be sold successfully to conservatives; this is why, when they are placed at the top of the ticket, they generally lose. Trying to sell RINOs to us is a losing proposition, and the epitome of stupidity! Give us a conservative janitor, a plumber, a sanitation worker—anybody but a RINO! We know janitors, plumbers, and sanitation workers who are fine people who agree with our politics—not so with RINOs. No more Democrats masquerading as conservative Republicans! We don't appreciate RINOs, FOX News pundits, or anybody else for that matter bashing our President. These folks obviously don't realize just how committed and loyal President Trump's supporters are. It seems preposterous that people still don't understand this, but perhaps it's possible—if they're in a coma! Vilifying President Trump and believing that his loyal supporters are going to desert him is truly the epitome of stupidity! There is a better chance of New Mexico becoming a tropical rainforest overnight than for that to happen.

All the defamatory attacks against Trump are absurd and show a lack of good judgment and common sense. Only the most callous radicals believe the nonsense anyway. Trying to change public opinion by bombarding us with hostile attacks is futile. The absurdity of the ill-conceived ambushes is laughable; President Trump and his supporters outsmart them every time!

Speaking of absurdity, probably the most absurd idea proposed and accepted by the human race has been circulating around the globe since 1859—the theory of Darwinian evolution!

By the 1870s, the scientific community and people who were educated beyond their level of intelligence claimed that evolution was a scientific fact. Many people today still accept the theory of evolution, although the "missing link" has never been found. Science experts examining fossil records cannot find a single transitional animal. No museum has been able to produce even one fossil of an intermediate animal. Charles Darwin, the author of the theory of evolution himself, indicated that for his theory to be correct, there would have to be numberless transitional animals. There were few fossil records available until after the death of Darwin. But by his own admission, if Darwin were alive today, he would likely refute his own theory of evolution. Yet many people still accept the theory as fact. Some people believe we evolved from apelike beings, sporting long arms for climbing and to help us balance ourselves—and we most likely lived in trees! While it's true that some people do act like animals and some animals do appear almost human, the evidence is certain— humans have always been humans, and animals have always been animals. God created them that way. The only creatures that are part animal and part man are in Greek mythology or the movies. Some of those who reject the theory of evolution believe life was started on our planet by aliens. Little green men far more intelligent than human beings came from outer space and created life on planet earth. If this were even remotely possible, then who created the little green men? Undoubtedly, these theories relieve atheists and other pagans of acknowledging God, the Creator. This is the epitome of stupidity!

Still, there are some individuals who sincerely believe in alien life forms on other planets, and some of these people believe aliens landed in the deserts of Arizona and New Mexico years ago. According to conspiracy theorists, an alien spacecraft crashed in the remote town of Roswell, New Mexico, in 1947. Although the government has debunked these claims, some people still believe little green men came to earth and have been hidden away by the United States military. Roswell hosts a UFO festival to celebrate the 1947 event each year. I assume the festival is hosted annually for entertainment purposes and the revenue the city garners from UFO enthusiasts.

I don't believe in aliens; however, the behavior of radical Democrats is so bizarre and hateful that I wonder from time to time if they could be the missing link or irate aliens from outer space disguised as Americans! One thing for sure is that the behavior of radical Democrats is the epitome of stupidity; it's impossible to behave any dumber than that!

What radicals apparently don't realize is that one day they'll be required to give an account for their misdeeds, for sowing strife, promoting hatred, and perverting justice. They will stand before the courts of heaven, where godly justice will be meted out. The Lord loves rebellious sinners, but that's not going to prevent His righteous judgment in the end. He asks people to consider their ways and repent now—before the coming final judgment!

CHAPTER 11

Justice Turned Backward

No one calls for justice, nor does any plead for truth.
They trust in empty words and speak lies;
they conceive evil and bring forth iniquity.

ISAIAH 59:4 NKJV

The Bible says that evil people don't understand justice, nor do they believe they should be subject to justice for their crimes and misdeeds. The wicked are confident they'll always escape punishment; justice being served doesn't apply to them. Also, many of the rich and powerful don't fear being brought to justice, especially corrupt politicians. Crooked politicians know that they're immune to law enforcement and the justice system that applies to everybody else. They can commit various crimes for which they'll never be prosecuted. They count on top law enforcement officials looking the other way on their behalf.

Generally, the only people who get convicted of crimes are conservatives; liberals normally are exempt from prosecution. In fact, conservatives sometimes get accused and convicted of a crime they haven't even committed. There are laws and rules for conservatives and ordinary citizens, but the same rules of justice don't apply to liberals—especially radical politicians. One set of rules applies for conservatives, and a vastly different set of rules applies to liberals and other radicals. Crooked politicians know there's a high probability of escaping prosecution.

Corrupt politicians know that if they're about to be exposed for heinous crimes that are politically or personally embarrassing, they can always hire an assassin to eliminate the pesky problem. High-profile politicians who have something horrific to hide aren't going to allow themselves to be outed, so they simply "eliminate the problem." They realize they can easily dispose of individuals who become liabilities without fear of punishment. They can break virtually any law with impunity—and odds are, people who have dirt on them, people like Jeffrey Epstein, will not live to see tomorrow!

They not only assassinate people's character, but if deemed necessary, they will also assassinate the nuisances standing in their way. This is simply the way things work in the political arena in the United States today. Unfortunately, it's also how things work in our justice system—the guilty often get off the hook scot-free. The idea of real justice being served generally doesn't apply to people on the left. Justice and *hyper-justice—or injustice*—is reserved strictly for those on the right.

Liberals aren't interested in objectivity and seeing justice executed. This is the reason people often accuse those who are innocent, while ignoring and excusing those who are guilty of crimes and gross misconduct. This is particularly true where partisan politics is concerned. Godless people reject equity and truth, and they condone and excuse the horrific behavior of those on the left. Guilty people on the left and those excusing them make a mockery of justice, righteousness, and truth. The Bible says in **Isaiah 59:14–15, "Justice is turned back. And righteousness stands afar off, for truth is fallen in the street, and equity cannot enter. So truth fails, and he who departs from evil makes himself a prey."** These verses describe what's happening in the realm of politics in our country today. Verse 14 indicates that justice, righteousness, and fairness will be in jeopardy when truth has been dispensed with by a people or a nation. Verse 15 indicates that when people amend their ways and depart from a path of unrighteousness, they'll become prey or enemies of evil men. These scriptures seem to apply fairly accurately in President Trump's case. If he was still a liberal Democrat with a radical agenda that would bring the United States to the brink of disaster, the left would demand he be vindicated. In fact, there would never have been an investigation into a *fabricated* Russian hoax or an *ill-contrived* impeachment probe in the first place. But now Donald Trump finds himself a despised enemy of wicked individuals, because he has committed the heinous crime of departing from and denouncing liberal ideology!

President Trump's crimes are that he dared question the policies of President Obama, and he soundly defeated the left's *darling* candidate, Hillary Clinton. For this, radicals everywhere are incensed still, and they desperately want the president impeached and removed from office for crimes he hasn't committed. The fact that he has done nothing wrong is immaterial; they just want to destroy his presidency and disenfranchise his voters. They know Hillary Clinton was guilty of mishandling classified information and jeopardizing our national security—but they don't care. They're angry, and they want to stay that way. They wanted their candidate to be elected, but they don't want justice to prevail.

Any reasonable person knows that President Trump didn't collude with the Russians, and that he isn't guilty of wrongdoing. And any rational person also knows that Clinton was guilty of failing to properly protect our national security, and she and the DNC also staged all kinds of underhanded tricks and acts of political violence to try to defeat Donald Trump. Then henchmen in the FBI, CIA, and other Deep State Justice Department officials tried to implicate him in crimes for which he wasn't guilty. This is the worst scandal and the most atrocious miscarriage of justice ever perpetuated upon a president or upon the citizens of the United States of America. The whole ugly, fabricated mess is a total travesty and a dark blemish on the character of top law enforcement officers in our country—along with some of their nasty minions. The Russian hoax and the impeachment absurdity have exposed the black hearts of both Democrats and RINOs in Congress, the media folks, and other individuals across the land. But these hoaxes and miscarriages of justice only make Trump supporters more committed and more determined than ever to see that he gets reelected in 2020.

There has been an extensive, expensive, and unjustified investigation involving President Trump and his campaign, but there has been a brief and seemingly *nonexistent* investigation into the clearly negligent and criminal behavior of Hillary Clinton. When she was the secretary of state, Clinton used her family's private email server, located in her home basement in New York, to conduct government business instead of using a secure government source. An FBI examination of Clinton's email server found over one hundred classified emails, some marked "Secret" and others "Top Secret," and over two thousand other emails not formerly marked classified that were later designated as such. These actions violated federal law, but FBI Director James Comey closed the investigation, calling her actions "extremely careless." I doubt that you or I would have received just a gentle tap on the wrist and such a generous investigative conclusion—that is, if you're a conservative like me. Clinton also used her unsecured BlackBerry frequently, even though she was warned repeatedly about the security risks. Another egregious act committed by Clinton was allowing individuals with no security clearance to manage her private server. In addition, the emails were at risk of being hacked and surveilled by foreign intelligence operatives; indeed, the server was hacked, but this was not reported to proper authorities. This reads like a spy novel with a very incompetent secretary of state at the helm. By the way, of the many classified documents possibly exposed to foreign entities and non-cleared individuals working for her, both Comey and Clinton claimed that her knowledge of classified markings wasn't sophisticated enough to understand the designation of the emails—incredible. When I was a mere E-4 in the army and hillbilly stupid, I understood how to identify classified markings and the importance of properly protecting government-sensitive documents. If Hillary didn't understand classified information, then why in the world was she ever appointed to be the secretary of state? Comey saw no issue with any of Clinton's misconduct—except carelessness—no problem here, moving on!

Yet, Trump and his associates were spied on and investigated for years, and they are still being harassed to this day because the investigation truly has never stopped, even though this investigation is based on questionable information and very suspect sources. Likewise, the illegitimate impeachment conducted by despicably dishonest Democrats is another example of a lack of integrity and a disregard for the rule of law by the left. This is justice turned backward and upside down—absolutely disgusting antics by Congress and the Justice Department!

For more information on the Russian hoax and collusion on the part of President Trump that never happened, I recommend reading *The Russian Hoax* by Gregg Jarrett, and *Spygate*, written by Dan Bongino. Bongino's latest book is called *Exonerated.* You may want to read it as well. You can also receive updated information from Dan by signing up for his email podcasts at newsletters@em.bongino.com. His newsletter and podcast are excellent sources of political information from a conservative perspective. Another great conservative source of information is Tom Fitton, at www.JudicialWatch.org. Bongino and Fitton will keep you up to date on all of the liberal nonsense and their seemingly never-ending fiendish plots.

Another devilish plot perpetrated by the left was the failed takedown of Supreme Court Justice Brett Kavanaugh. He was the victim of a cruel plot to keep him from being confirmed as a United States Supreme Court Justice; he was much too conservative for the hounds of hell. Watching his confirmation hearing was like watching a horror movie, or the latest version of *Sharks in the Water*! It was truly a despicable display of U.S. Senate partisan politics at its worst. The only other congressional event that even came close was the attempted takedown of Justice Clarence Thomas during his confirmation hearing in 1991. During the Kavanaugh hearing, the left employed Christine Ford (clearly a very disturbed woman) to testify against Brett Kavanaugh. Many folks in the media claimed she was a credible witness, but she didn't appear very credible or believable from my living room sofa! The whole ugly display of the attempted character assassination of Kavanaugh blemished forever the character of Senate Democrats in the eyes of many people. One of my sisters who is apolitical was shocked by the actions of these partisan hacks. She went so far as to say, "They raped that man!"

Other patriotic Americans who've been "raped and pillaged" by the left include Navy Seal Eddie Gallagher, Dinesh D'Souza, Sharyl Attkisson, James Rosen, and many founders of conservative nonprofit organizations, to name a few. Navy Seal Gallagher, who has been deployed to Iraq and Afghanistan eight times, was accused of war crimes, not for raping and maiming innocent women and children, but for supposedly murdering an ISIS terrorist! How exactly does one "murder" an ISIS terrorist? Gallagher was acquitted on the charge of murder, but he was convicted of a lesser crime and reduced in rank. He was all but crucified by those on the left. This kind of mistreatment makes me wonder why anybody would want to serve in our military nowadays. Thankfully, President Trump pardoned Gallagher and had his rank restored!

Dinesh D'Souza also is despised by the radical left. His major crime was producing videos criticizing the policies of President Obama and Hillary Clinton. The federal government was relentless in their pursuit of him, and they were finally able to convict him of the heinous crime of donating $20,000 to a friend's political campaign. Dinesh was charged with violating campaign finance laws—but you won't ever see this happening to anyone on the left. I recommend reading this godly man's books; he's a true conservative with a great intellectual mind. This is another reason the radicals hate him so much; they're seriously threatened by intellect!

Journalists Sharyl Attkisson and James Rosen were also targets of an unscrupulous Justice Department investigation under the Obama administration. By the way, Sharyl is an excellent investigative reporter and the host of the television show *Full Measure*. Another group that was targeted during the Obama administration were the conservative nonprofits. While conservative nonprofit groups suffered from lost revenue, the grievous targeter working for the IRS got to remain in her cushy job and retire with a very generous pension. Justice truly is turned upside down in the United States.

These cases are just a few of the many examples of justice turned backward in the United States. We cannot trust justice in the hands or courts of radicals. Unjust shenanigans are routine fare for them, and those injured by their cruel, baseless accusations are always conservatives. All the cases of injustice perpetuated against conservatives by radical Democrats sends a clear message of caution to conservatives to always be on guard when it comes to justice in the United States. Conservatives aren't likely to experience fairness.

Radicals always expose even the slightest imagined flaw of conservatives, while hiding the major flaws of ungodly Democrats. They overlook or camouflage the criminal behavior of their candidates and trusted friends. Radicals also consistently express admiration for individuals of questionable character; they appear drawn to people with little or no integrity. In 2018 and the first half of 2019, far-left radicals were exuberantly praising the merits of Michael Avenatti and promoting him as a serious contender for the presidency—oops, until... The disgraced lawyer was charged with bank fraud, tax evasion, embezzlement, trying to extort $25 million from Nike, and then he was essentially barred from practicing law in California; at that point, they reluctantly changed their minds.

Michael Avenatti, Jeffrey Epstein, and Bill Clinton are the kind of men the left find appealing. They also appear very fond of violent protestors, terrorists such as Iranian General Qasem Soleimani, or anyone opposing law and order. Some of their greatest heroes are those who escape justice.

The Bible says in Psalm 12:8, "The wicked prowl on every side, when vileness is exalted among the sons of men." This scripture fairly accurately describes the actions of the radical left today. Depravity is acceptable, and immoral people who lack ethical character and are able to circumvent justice are honored as some of their most revered heroes.

CHAPTER 12

Defining Heroes

Greater love has no one than this,
that one lay down his life for his friends.
JOHN 15:13 NASB

True heroes are selfless individuals who are willing to risk their reputations and sacrifice their lives for the benefit of others or an honorable cause. But the radical left tries to cheapen their sacrifice by bestowing hero status upon undeserving and even villainous individuals, while vilifying great conservative heroes. They are shameless in the way they politicize stories and misrepresent facts to convince the public that military deserters, savage thugs, violent protestors, civil rights extortionists, evil dictators, terrorists, and other people of questionable character are somehow esteemed, courageous heroes. Radicals are adept at misleading people and creating heroes where none exist. By using deception, they've managed to change the definition of the word *hero*. They hail many individuals as heroes who have experienced extraordinary circumstances—much of which was self-imposed—such as individuals who crossed the border illegally, notorious criminals, and unpatriotic deserters who have become prisoners of war.

Conservatives view things differently. A person's circumstances don't necessarily make them a hero. Most heroes are distinguished from ordinary citizens, not so much by their circumstances, but how they react during unfavorable conditions. A hero often disregards his or her own safety to rescue others in dangerous situations. The Lord Jesus Christ is the ultimate Hero! He sacrificed everything for us even though He knew many people would reject His sacrifice. The life of Christ and His sacrifice exemplifies the perfect illustration of a hero. The far left has tried to redefine what it means to be a hero, but conservatives aren't buying their modernized definition.

One dictionary definition of a *hero* is "a person who is admired or idealized for courage, outstanding achievements, or noble qualities." Another definition is "an individual who risks his or her own life for the good of others or to save the life of others." Still another definition of a *hero* is "a person of distinguished courage or ability, admired for his or her brave deeds and noble qualities." My definition of a hero is "a person who risks or sacrifices his or her life or reputation to save others from physical or spiritual death; a person of courage and good moral character who is willing to relinquish his or her own comfort for the furtherance of the Gospel of Jesus Christ." This is my definition of a hero; it's also, in my opinion, the best definition. By my definition or the definitions found in various dictionaries, the United States and many other countries have been honored with a vast number of heroes. Many ordinary citizens become heroes and heroines almost daily, but most heroes aren't remembered by name for very long. Other heroes are never known by name at all. Many of them come from average families without the benefit of fame or family name recognition. Many of our military heroes are nameless people who've fought in various wars and sacrificially given their lives for the rest of us; some are buried in unmarked graves and all but forgotten except for a few family members who keep their memory alive.

The United States has had many military heroes, some recognized and some not, but far too many to mention. It's not my intent to provide an in-depth review of military heroes, so I'll only mention a few of the more notable ones. It also is not my intent to cover every war or conflict in our nation's history. I purposely won't address recognized heroes of the Civil War, since many of them wouldn't meet the qualifications of my definition of *hero*. Though one hero who did stand out, during the Civil War was President Abraham Lincoln, but I will address his role later, along with other civil rights activists. Many people who fought in the Civil War were clearly fighting to keep slavery, while others were fighting to abolish it. Still others were fighting strictly to protect their families and preserve their farms and way of life. They were neither fighting for or against slavery; they primarily were engaged in the battle for self-preservation. With this being the case, some of the lines were blurred as to what some citizens were actually fighting for. For this and the reason mentioned above, I won't address recognized heroes of the Civil War. I also won't name individual heroes involved in the American Indian Wars or the Spanish-American War and other lesser conflicts, but I will begin with the American Revolution.

Before I dive into the Revolutionary War, however, I would like to briefly mention the contributions made by African American troops in the Civil War, Indian Wars, and Spanish-American War. Many blacks fought courageously in the Civil War, with twenty-five troops winning Medals of Honor for their heroics. Black troops in the Indian Wars earned a total of eighteen Medals of Honor for valor, fourteen of which were awarded to Buffalo soldiers. Six blacks won Medals of Honor for their bravery in the Spanish-American War, five medals of which went to Buffalo soldiers. Black troops were segregated from white regiments until 1948, after the end of World War II. Black soldiers were also reluctantly allowed to participate in the Revolutionary War, some of whom won their freedom after the war's conclusion. Imagine fighting for a country where one is a slave!

One outstanding hero during the American Revolution was Nathan Hale, a soldier and spy for the Continental Army during the American Revolutionary War. But while he was participating in an intelligence-gathering mission in New York, he was captured by the British and executed. One of his most famous quotes was this: "*I only regret that I have but one life to lose for my country.*"[10] Imagine that kind of selflessness and exceptional valor! A few other courageous men who have historically been recognized as

Revolutionary War heroes are George Washington, Henry Knox, Nathanael Greene, John Stark, Daniel Morgan, Anthony Wayne, and Paul Revere. Even Benedict Arnold was considered a Revolutionary War hero until he became a traitor and sold out his own country!

Benedict Arnold is one of those individuals who started well but didn't finish well. Arnold should not be recognized as a hero, because he obviously was a man who lacked integrity and good moral character. He also was unpatriotic, selling out his country for a few British pounds. There were a vast number of heroes and patriots, both men and women, whose actions were instrumental in winning our independence, but Benedict Arnold was not one of them. Once considered a patriot, he became a traitor who cherished money and self-promotion more than his own country. When he was caught spying for the enemy, he fled to the British side and fought with their troops. He was a traitor in the worst sense of the word because he fought with British soldiers against the American troops whom he once had commanded in the Continental Army—truly a shockingly abhorrent act!

Perhaps the most notable hero of World War I was Sergeant Alvin York. The movie *Sergeant York* gives an account of his life and heroics; the movie is definitely worth watching. The movie about York's life is a very stirring and touching story. He exhibited extraordinary bravery and was one of the most decorated U.S. Army soldiers of World War I. Sergeant York was awarded the Congressional Medal of Honor, the Distinguished Service Cross, and several other citations for valor. He received the Medal of Honor for leading an attack on a German machine gun site and he has been credited with killing twenty-five enemy soldiers. He also almost single-handedly captured over 130 enemy combatants. He was a very poor lad from the hills of Tennessee who initially claimed conscientious objector status, but he was eventually persuaded that participating in a war wouldn't violate his faith. Surely, Alvin York must have come to realize that the Lord had armed him with strength for battle and had subdued his enemies under his feet (see 2 Samuel 22:40). Sergeant York was a Christian man of stellar character, and he was just one of the many true-life heroes who fought in World War I.

A few other extraordinary men and Medal of Honor winners of World War I were Lieutenant Colonel Charles Whittlesey, Captain Eddie Rickenbacker, Lieutenant Frank Luke, Lieutenant Edouard Izac, Sergeant Major Daniel Daly, Sergeant Henry Johnson, and Private John J. Kelly. Captain Rickenbacker was a Medal of Honor winner and the most decorated fighter pilot in WWI. Sergeant Major Daly won two Medals of Honor, plus several other medals for valor. There were hundreds of heroes and many Congressional Medal of Honor winners in World War I. Many of our soldiers, sailors, airmen, and marines not only were awarded Medals of Honor but numerous other medals for valor as well. Many heroes were awarded their medals posthumously. We have long been a country of valiant war heroes.

The most legendary hero of World War II was Audie Leon Murphy. He was the most decorated American combat soldier of World War II. He received every military combat award for valor available from the U.S. Army, including the Medal of Honor, as well as French and Belgian awards for heroism. Audie Murphy was a true war hero. He began his military service in 1942 as an enlisted man, but he was promoted to the rank of second lieutenant and subsequently first lieutenant during the war. He later also served in the Army Reserves and the Army National Guard and ended his military service with the rank of major. Unfortunately, Murphy suffered from what is known today as post-traumatic stress disorder. He once said, *"No soldier ever really survives a war."*[11] He was plagued with frequent nightmares and insomnia, and evidently he also suffered from guilt related to the war. Murphy later became a well-known film actor and songwriter. He has a star on the Hollywood Walk of Fame. My husband and I still enjoy his movies today.

Audie Murphy was born in Texas to a poor sharecropper family, the seventh of twelve children. He had this to say when describing his childhood: *"It was a full-time job just existing."*[12] (By the way, that was my sentiment exactly when growing up in rural Kentucky!) Murphy tried to join the military when he was seventeen years old, but he was rejected by both the army and the marines. His age and his small five-foot-five, 112-pound frame probably had something to do with both services rejecting him. He reapplied for military service when he was eighteen, but he was turned down once again by the Marine Corps, but then he was accepted by the U.S. Army. Murphy's feats as a war hero were quite amazing. His autobiography is captured in his book, *To Hell and Back*. Also, his autobiography was subsequently made into a movie by the same name—and it was the highest-grossing film for Universal Studios for many years.

Again, Audie Murphy was just one of many heroes of World War II. There were many others who also displayed great bravery and distinguished themselves as war heroes. Darby's Rangers (named for Brigadier General William Orlando Darby) and Merrill's Marauders (named for Brigadier General Frank Merrill) certainly served with distinction. The daring exploits of both the Darby Rangers and Merrill Marauders were made into motion pictures. Several other war heroes and Medal of Honor recipients from WWII were Colonel Gregory "Pappy" Boyington and Colonel Lewis Millett; First Lieutenants Vernon Baker, John R. Fox, and Charles Thomas; Master Sergeant Woodrow Keeble, a Native American who also served in the Korean War; Staff Sergeants Edward Carter Jr. and Rubin Rivers; Private First Class (PFC) Willy James and Private George Watson. Again, there are far too many WWII heroes to list. Many of them earned not only Medals of Honor, but Purple Hearts and a whole host of other medals for bravery as well.

Colonel Pappy Boyington was a World War II ace combat pilot whose valor earned him a Congressional Medal of Honor, a Navy Cross, and a Purple Heart. He was credited with destroying twenty-eight enemy planes. Although he was a little rough around the edges, he was a courageous military man, and he was beloved by his men, who nicknamed him "Pappy" due to his age. He wrote an autobiography titled *Baa Baa Black Sheep*, which later resulted in a television series by that name. (Note: In syndication the TV series was renamed *Black Sheep Squadron*.) His character was played by actor Robert Conrad of Wild, Wild West fame.

Master Sergeant Woodrow Wilson Keeble was a Native American who fought bravely in both WWII and the Korean War. He was a member of the Army National Guard of North Dakota, before being called to active duty by the U.S. Army, and he distinguished himself particularly in the Korean War as a seasoned combat veteran. He risked his life to save his fellow soldiers, for which he received several medals, including four Purple Hearts for being wounded in both WWII and the Korean War. He also was awarded the Medal of Honor posthumously, and he was the first full-blooded Sioux Indian to receive such an honor.

Corporal Mitchell Red Cloud Jr. was yet another Native American who fought with distinction both in World War II and then in the Korean War. Red Cloud first entered the United States Marine Corps and was honorably discharged after WWII with the rank of sergeant. He subsequently reenlisted, but this time in the army, and he fought in the Korean War. He was killed in action during the Korean War, during which his heroic actions earned him a Medal of Honor, awarded posthumously. He also was awarded two Purple Hearts. He single-handedly held off Chinese troops to save his unit from a surprise attack. Red Cloud was shot eight times, but he still continued to engage in battle. He asked a fellow soldier to tie him upright to a tree so he could continue fighting while the men in his unit retreated. He was found the next morning surrounded by many dead enemy soldiers. Corporal Red Cloud has several sites named after him, plus a street and a park, and a ship was christened in his name. The Ho-Chunk Nation honors him every July Fourth by observing Corporal Mitchell Red Cloud Jr. Day. He is also featured among other Korean War heroes in a documentary film called *Finnigan's War.*

A few other heroes from the Korean War who stand out with distinction and should be recognized are Colonel Lewis Millett (who also served in WWII and the Vietnam War); Sergeant First Class Tony Burris; Corporal Tibor (Ted) Rubin; and PFCs William Henry Thompson, Jack Hanson, Herbert Pilila'au, Anthony Kaho'ohanohano, and Demensio Rivera.

Colonel Lewis Millett served honorably in three wars and was awarded a Medal of Honor for his valor in the Battle of Bayonet Hill in Korea. He actually received a total of four Medals of Honor, a Purple Heart, and a long list of other medals during his distinguished military career. He was wounded in the Battle of Bayonet Hill, but he refused to be evacuated until the hill was secured. Lewis Millett joined the Army National Guard while still in high school in 1938. When President FDR initially indicated he had no plans to get involved in WWII, Millett became impatient and deserted to Canada, where he joined the Canadian Army. From there he was shipped to England for training. After America entered WWII, he rejoined the United States Army and fought bravely along with other U.S. troops. He later was court-martialed for desertion, but the court martial was quickly forgotten and he was promoted to Second Lieutenant. He was recognized for his gallantry in all three wars in which he served, and he won a number of both U.S. and international medals. Colonel Millett has a road at Osan Air Base, South Korea, and a park in San Jacinto, California, named in his honor. Lewis Millett is the kind of military deserter (not a traitor) whom all of us can honor and be proud of—a true American hero!

Yet another great American hero is Corporal Tibor (Ted) Rubin. His story is extraordinary in that he was held as a prisoner of war twice, once as a Hungarian civilian and Holocaust survivor and the second time as a United States military soldier in North Korea. Ted Rubin was held for fourteen months in the notorious Mauthausen Concentration Camp in Austria, before being liberated by U.S. combat troops. In 1948, Rubin immigrated to the United States. To show his gratitude for being rescued by American forces, Rubin joined the United States Army after immigrating to the States. (His father, stepmother, and two sisters did not survive the Holocaust.) After enlisting in the army, Rubin fought bravely in the Korean War. His heroic actions saved a number of men in his unit from sure death. Just one of his many heroic sacrifices was holding a hilltop single-handedly and guarding a road while his unit retreated to safety. Rubin was later severely wounded in battle and captured, becoming a prisoner of war for thirty months. During that time, he selflessly risked his life on numerous occasions to secure food to keep other POWs alive. Rubin was awarded two Purple Hearts and a Medal of Honor for his bravery. He is one of the Korean War heroes included in the documentary film *Finnigan's War*.

Six great Americans heroes who gave their all during the Korean War and are recognized for their valiant last stands are Sergeant First Class Tony Burris, PFC William Henry Thompson, PFC Jack Hanson, PFC Anthony Kaho'ohanohano, PFC Herbert Pilila'au, and PFC Demensio Rivera. These men killed many enemy soldiers by their heroic actions, keeping other American troops alive to fight another day. Their stories, though heart-wrenching, should be read and appreciated by all Americans. All of these men are heroic Purple Heart and Medal of Honor recipients. Some of these men and other troops (both American and French) experienced some of the fiercest fighting against the Communists in mountainous terrain. One of these battles became known as Bloody Ridge, and a month long battle was later called Heartbreak Ridge, where casualties were high on both sides. The remaining heroes from the Korean War are far too many to identify in this book. Again, I recommend that all patriotic Americans read the history of the Korean War and the touching stories of our many military heroes.

The next major conflict was the Vietnam War; it certainly had its fair share of true-life heroes—far, far too many to identify, so I'll mention only a few. Over 58,000 troops died in the Vietnam War. A war memorial in their honor is erected at the National Mall in Washington, D.C. Unfortunately, the returning troops from Vietnam were met with animus from ruthless fellow citizens rather than receiving a hero's welcome home. Liberal celebrities and misguided students showed contempt for our brave American heroes, both during and after the war. Not only did these valiant men have to fight an unpopular war, enduring inhumane treatment at the hands of the enemy, but those who survived also had to suffer wounds from merciless fellow Americans upon their return to the United States. (Incidentally, my father-in-law fought in both the Korean and Vietnam wars.)

Many heroes sacrificed their lives in the Vietnam War to save their comrades. They were awarded Purple Hearts, Medals of Honor, as well as other medals posthumously for their gallantry. Just a few of those heroes are Sergeant First Class Eugene Ashley Jr.; Staff Sergeants Laszlo Rabel and Karl Taylor Sr.; Sergeant Ted Belcher; Lance Corporals Richard Anderson, Jedh Colby Barker, and Kenneth Worley; Specialist Four Robert Stryker; PFCs James Anderson Jr. (the first black marine to receive the Medal of Honor), Oscar Austin, John Barnes III, Leslie Allen Bellrichard, Bruce Carter, and Ralph Dias.

Perhaps two of the most famous men serving in the Vietnam War whom most folks honor as heroes were Vice Admiral James Bond Stockdale and Captain John Sidney McCain III. Both were held as prisoners of war in Vietnam. Vice Admiral Stockdale was the highest-ranking navy officer to become a prisoner of war in Vietnam, and he spent seven and a half years in captivity. He was one of eleven prisoners known as the Alcatraz Gang. Because these guys resisted their captors and encouraged others to do the same, they became known as resistance leaders. Their punishment for resistance was solitary confinement in tiny windowless cells, where they were locked in leg irons at night. Both Stockdale and McCain were held in the infamous Hanoi Hilton, where they and fellow POWs suffered brutal beatings and torture. Meanwhile, back on the home front, Stockdale's wife, Sybil, organized the League of American Families of POWs and MIAs, with the assistance of other wives and servicemen, to draw attention to the harsh treatment suffered by prisoners of war in Vietnam. The league prompted the then-president and Congress to acknowledge and address the gross mistreatment of prisoners. Fortunately, Vice Admiral Stockdale survived captivity, and much later ran unsuccessfully for vice president of the United States in 1992 on the Independent Party ticket. Several structures have been named in his honor. Vice Admiral Stockdale was awarded two Purple Hearts, a Medal of Honor, and numerous other medals for heroism.

Captain McCain also was fortunate to survive over five years as a prisoner of war. McCain was awarded a Purple Heart and several other medals for his military service. After serving two terms as a United States Representative, he was elected to the U.S. Senate in 1987. McCain served in the capacity of U.S. senator until his death in August 2018. McCain also ran unsuccessfully for president of the United States in 2008. He was the recipient of not only military honors, but many civilian awards as well. He also authored a number of books. After his death, he received a hero's sendoff, both in the nation's capital and in his home state of Arizona. (While I greatly appreciate the military service of both McCain and Stockdale, I didn't always agree with them on political and social issues. I especially opposed Stockdale's pro-choice stance.)

It's not my intent to promote anyone as more heroic due to their fame or name recognition, because just the opposite could be true. Many individuals who served and died without being recognized might actually have been more heroic. Many of our greatest heroes may have died in battle, and others died in captivity without ever being widely recognized for their heroism.

Another valiant soldier who served in the Vietnam War was Captain Humbert "Rocky" Versace. He volunteered for a six-month extension to his tour of duty, but he was injured in battle, captured, and became a prisoner of war just two weeks before the completion of his tour. Captain Versace made four attempts to escape, but he was never successful. He was executed by his captors, the Viet Cong, and his body has never been recovered. He had planned to attend seminary at the end of his military service and later become a Catholic priest. He also had planned to return to Vietnam as a missionary working with orphans. Captain Versace was awarded a Purple Heart and Medal of Honor for his bravery. This man was truly a great American hero! Had he survived, he undoubtedly would have been a great priest and a first-rate missionary as well.

One of the most decorated veterans of the Vietnam War is Staff Sergeant Joe Ronnie Hooper. He was credited with killing 115 enemy soldiers; he was wounded eight times during the war, but he survived to fight another day. Hooper was awarded eight Purple Hearts, a Medal of Honor, and a whole host of other medals for his extreme heroism during the war. He later became a commissioned officer and attained the rank of captain, while serving in the United States Army Reserves.

Another veteran serving during the Korean and Vietnam Wars who bears recognition is Navy Commander Helen Maznio. She was a nurse who served honorably for twenty-four years, lived a very frugal life, and left five million dollars to the Navy-Marine Corps Relief Society upon her death at age ninety-two. The Relief Society provides emergency financial assistance to active duty and retired U. S. Navy and Marine Corps personnel. Commander Maznio considered the Navy-Marine Corps her family, so she chose to leave a valuable inheritance to her beloved family.

This brings us to the next major conflicts, the Afghanistan War and the Iraq War on terrorism. Again, there are many heroes from both of these conflicts, but I'll only mention those who are Medal of Honor winners. As of the writing of this book, there are currently fourteen Medal of Honor recipients who survived the Afghanistan War, and four who were killed in combat. The names of those fortunate enough to survive are Command Master Chief Edward Byers, Staff Sergeant Ty Carter, Corporal Kyle Carpenter, Staff Sergeant Salvatore Giunta, Captain Florent Groberg, Sergeant Dakota Meyer, Master Sergeant Leroy Petry, Staff Sergeant Ryan Pitts, Staff Sergeant Clinton Romesha, Staff Sergeant Ronald Shurer, Navy Seal Master Chief Britt Slabinski, Major William Swenson, Sergeant Kyle White, and Sergeant Major Matthew Williams. All but two of these men also received Purple Hearts along with Medals of Honor and numerous other medals as well. Staff Sergeant Ronald Shurer survived the war, but later he lost his battle to cancer in May 2020. The four combat Medal of Honor heroes who were casualties of the Afghanistan War were Master Sergeant John Chapman, Staff Sergeant Robert James Miller, Sergeant First Class Jared Christopher Monti, and Navy Seal Lieutenant Michael Murphy. These men were awarded not only Medals of Honor, but Purple Hearts and numerous other medals as well.

One hero who gave his all in the Afghanistan War was Special Operations Master Sergeant John Chapman. He essentially chose to sacrifice himself, still engaging the enemy though he was badly wounded, to save the lives of his teammates. He is the first airman since the Vietnam War to be awarded the Medal of Honor. He also was the first Air Force Combat Controller to earn the Air Force Cross in any war in our history. He not only was a war hero, but a great father to his two daughters. Back in his high school yearbook, he had written: *"Give of yourself before taking from someone else,"*[13] and this quotation shows his selfless character.

There is only one surviving Iraq War Medal of Honor winner, Staff Sergeant David Bellavia, and five Medal of Honor recipients who were killed in action. Staff Sergeant Travis William Atkins was killed while shielding other comrades from an insurgent's explosive vest. Corporal Jason Lee Dunham, Specialist Ross Andrew McGinnis, and Navy Seal Master at Arms Second Class Michael Anthony Monsoor were all killed while smothering enemy grenades with their bodies. Sergeant First Class Paul Ray Smith was a seasoned veteran who fought in the Persian Gulf War, the Bosnian War, the Kosovo War, and the Iraq War. He was killed in Iraq during a fierce gun battle. SFC Smith had written to his parents these selfless words: *"There are two ways to come home, stepping off the plane and being carried off the plane. It doesn't matter how I come home, because I'm prepared to give all that I am to ensure all my boys make it home."*[14] This handsome, brave, seasoned combat veteran was only thirty-three years old!

Most of our war heroes are very young, even those who are experienced in war. And far too many of them come home carried off of a plane. Others walk off the plane, but they are badly wounded, either physically or emotionally—or both. Some of our heroes are badly disfigured, and some of them, such as Afghanistan War veteran Sergeant Johnny "Joey" Jones (whom I admire), are double amputees or worse, but they somehow readjust to the cruel blow life has dealt them and continue on with their lives. Sadly, many of our returning heroes choose not to go on with their lives. Selfless war veterans are my heroes—not disgruntled protest groupies, criminals, corrupt politicians, or wimpy rich college kids cowering in safe places because of some imagined wrong done to them!

There are numerous generals and far too many other military troops in various wars who earned the title of hero—too many to cite in this book. As I studied many of their stories, I was sincerely touched by their valor and selfless sacrifices. We owe our heroes a great debt of gratitude, which can never be repaid. Thousands gave their all. Many sacrificed their lives by smothering grenades or mines with their bodies, while others continued fighting while severely wounded, denying medical treatment until the battle was won. And many heroes charged ahead, where less courageous people would have retreated or fled. I encourage people to do their own research on our country's war history and read the gallant stories of the many heroes who served our country honorably and bravely—heroes recognized and honored by conservatives.

Our country also has produced many heroic first responders. On September 11, 2001, many police officers and firemen distinguished themselves as true heroes during one of the saddest days in our country's history. First responders, especially law enforcement officers, continue to serve often without much appreciation from a sometimes-hostile public. Hostility toward police officers is stoked by liberal politicians and the media when they indicate cops are culpable and criminals are misunderstood victims. Law enforcement officers have been harassed at places of business (some refusing to serve them), threatened in the streets, and made to feel like second-class citizens by thugs and irate radicals. (I realize there are some rogue police officers but the vast majority of police officers are honorable people, risking their lives on a daily basis to serve and protect the rest of us.)

The Bible says in Ecclesiastes 8:11, "When a crime is not punished quickly, people feel it is safe to do wrong" (NLT). Radicals feel it's safe to be antagonistic toward law enforcement, because they know they'll probably suffer no adverse consequences. Many of them view cops as evil, but police officers can rest assured that their sacrifice is valued and greatly respected by conservatives—in spite of top cops in the Obama administration being dirty and tainting their honorable profession. Radicals also accuse U.S. Immigration and Customs

Enforcement (ICE) and border patrol agents of being villains. Our country's courageous first responders and brave ICE and border patrol agents walk "through the valley of the shadow of death" on a regular basis; conservatives recognize this and honor them for both their patriotism and their heroism.

Another group of professionals that may be hailed as heroes is that of the space explorers, who've gone where few have gone before them. Imagine what it must be like in outer space, observing the earth and planets from a new perspective. If any of the space explorers were Christians, surely Psalm 147:4 must have come to mind. It reads, "He counts the number of the stars; He calls them all by name." Other scriptures that might have come to the minds of brave space explorers are Psalm 8:1 and Psalm 19:1. Psalm 8:1 reads, "O LORD, our Lord, how excellent is Your name in all the earth, who have set Your glory above the heavens!" And Psalm 19:1 reads, "The heavens declare the glory of God; and the firmament shows His handiwork."

Yes, space exploration is definitely an honorable profession with a list of heroes. Our president is definitely an advocate of space exploration, and he has been responsible for revitalizing space programs that were formerly decimated by the Obama administration. President Trump has also created another branch of the military called the Space Force, which will enhance our security and presence in space; this makes him a hero for promoting space exploration!

Our country has also been fortunate to produce wonderful civil rights heroes. One of the first civil rights activists was President Abraham Lincoln, who gave his life for the cause. President Lincoln was a godly Republican whom liberals hated and vilified until the day of his death—and then, there in his coffin, he suddenly became a great American hero! Until Lincoln was assassinated, he was met with great furor from liberals and other citizens who didn't want slavery to be abolished—but rather wanted it expanded. He was not the first, but one of the first civil rights heroes.

Another great American civil rights hero was Sojourner Truth. She was born into slavery in New York, but she escaped with her infant daughter in 1826. She was an abolitionist, a women's rights activist, a preacher, an author, and a great speech orator. Sojourner Truth went to court in 1828 to recover her son; she was the first black woman to win a case against a white man! She also helped recruit black troops for the Union Army. Sojourner Truth not only has a lengthy list of accomplishments, but she also has a prolific list of honors. She has been honored in numerous ways including having a U.S. postage stamp issued to honor her, as well as public schools and various other buildings, plus a highway and many other things named in her honor. Sculptures, murals, and monuments of her have been placed in several locations throughout the country as well. Truth was also recognized by *Smithsonian* magazine and was included in its list of the 100 Most Significant Americans of All Time, and she has been inducted into both the National and Michigan Women's Halls of Fame.

Yet another civil rights hero was Harriet Tubman. She is possibly the best-known abolitionist. She was born into slavery in Maryland, but she later escaped to freedom in the North. Ms. Tubman became a famous conductor of the Underground Railroad, and she helped several slaves escape to freedom prior to the start of the Civil War. Harriet Tubman earned the nickname "Moses" due to her rescue efforts in freeing her people. During the Civil War, she joined the Union Army as a nurse, and she worked as a scout and spy behind enemy lines. She helped the Union Army rescue seven hundred slaves in South Carolina on one mission. Tubman also later traveled extensively, promoting women's suffrage. She was buried with military honors at the Fort Hill Cemetery in Auburn, New York.

Harriet Tubman and Reverend Dr. Martin Luther King Jr. are without a doubt my favorite civil rights heroes. I studied their lives—and became very fond of both of them—in a Black History class in college. I studied the speeches of Dr. Martin Luther King in my Political Science class in college as well. To me, no more eloquent speech has ever been given than "I Have a Dream." King's speech still touches me very deeply even today. He perhaps was the best orator of our time. Who can forget the famous words, "I have a dream that one day…let freedom ring; and free at last!

Free at last! Thank God Almighty, we are free at last!"? Who can forget awe-inspiring phrases such as these? Not me! I still weep almost uncontrollably when I read the speech or study the life of Dr. Martin Luther King Jr. I remember when I was a young girl how much I wanted to travel to Alabama and march with Dr. Martin Luther King in the civil rights movement.

Dr. Martin Luther King, like President Lincoln, sacrificed his life for civil rights. King was impressive, even from early childhood. He was a gifted student; he skipped two grades in school, and he started college at the age of fifteen years young. Reverend King was a political activist and a Baptist minister by trade. He stood for justice and called for peace, and he's one of my favorite people in American history. This brilliant man's life was cut short in 1968 by an assassin's bullet. As might be expected, his murder caused rioting and violence in many cities across the country. The night before he was shot, King spoke words that sounded almost like a premonition or a foretelling of his impending death. But Martin Luther King, like President Lincoln, didn't seem to fear death. I think they relied on God's Word for comfort, and most likely they trusted in scriptures such as Isaiah 26:3 and Psalm 17:15. Isaiah 26:3 says, "You will keep in perfect peace all who trust in you, all whose thoughts are fixed on you" (NLT). Psalm 17:15 reads, "As for me, I will see Your face in righteousness; I shall be satisfied when I awake in Your likeness." (Psalm 17:15 is one of my many favorite scriptures.)

Today people still question whether the assassin who killed King acted alone. The memory of Dr. King's life is honored every year in January as a national holiday. In 1983, President Ronald Reagan signed a bill into law creating a national holiday to honor Reverend Dr. Martin Luther King Jr. I encourage everyone to reread the "I Have a Dream" speech by Dr. King, then read a more detailed history of his life and contributions to civil rights. Unlike many *self-proclaimed* civil rights activists of today, Dr. Martin Luther King Jr. was a true American hero!

Dr. King's civil rights hero was a former slave and a Methodist minister named Richard Allen. I think Dr. King would be embarrassed by and greatly disappointed with the radical actions of modern-day civil rights leaders.

The last group of heroes we should express honor and appreciation for comes from the Christian community. Like our many military warriors, there simply are too many Christian heroes to list or address in this book. Our country and other countries around the world certainly have been blessed with numerous champions of the faith; I'll only mention a few of them. Two of our more recent heroes who certainly deserve our honor, respect, and recognition are Reverend Billy Graham and Mother Teresa.

Billy Graham was an extraordinary man who needs no introduction. He is one of the most influential Christian leaders of our time, and he is known and beloved internationally. He and the Holy Spirit were responsible for leading millions of people to faith in Christ through television and radio broadcasts, both indoor and outdoor rallies, and evangelistic crusades. Billy Graham's sincere Christian compassion and ministry touched millions of people's lives here and abroad. He was an advisor to a number of U.S. presidents and a promoter of civil rights. His ministry (the Billy Graham Evangelistic Association) has served both the physical and spiritual needs of millions of people for more than six decades, and it continues to serve them today. We owe a great debt of gratitude to Reverend Graham; his wife, Ruth Bell Graham; his son Franklin; his grandson Will; and other family members who continue to carry the torch for Christ. They are true heroes of the faith! After Graham's death in 2018 at age ninety-nine, he became the fourth civilian to lie in state at the United States Capitol rotunda in Washington, D.C. (Incidentally, the only news network that gave Reverend Graham's multiple funeral services adequate airtime and showed him the respect he so aptly deserved was FOX News. Many of us are thankful to FOX executives for their godly wisdom and reverence for this great American hero.) Billy Graham provided us with a number of memorable quotes, including the following:

"Courage is contagious. When a brave man takes a stand, the spines of others are often stiffened."

"I've read the last page of the Bible. It's all going to turn out all right."

"My home is in heaven. I'm just traveling through this world."[15]

The testimony of Billy Graham and all heroes of the faith is undoubtedly expressed by the words in Psalm 119:161b–162. These verses read, "My heart stands in awe of Your word. I rejoice at Your word, as one who finds great treasure." All faith heroes have publicly demonstrated their love for Christ and how much they cherish the Word of God.

Another hero of our Christian faith is Mother Teresa. This diminutive lady took a vow of poverty to live and work among the poorest of the poor, ministering to both the spiritual and the physical needs of thousands of people in India. She rescued *discarded* people from horrendous circumstances, ministered the Gospel to them, and helped them live and die with dignity. Her Missionaries of Charity ministry has provided health, food, family counseling, orphanages, and other services to millions of people in India and numerous other countries. She is the recipient of a number of honorary awards, and she won the Nobel Peace Prize in 1979. Mother Teresa has provided us with a number of memorable quotes, some of which essentially say if your motives are *misunderstood* or your efforts *aren't appreciated—do it anyway!*

Both Reverend Billy Graham and Mother Teresa were prolific writers. Another prolific writer, and one of my favorite authors and Christian heroes, is Watchman Nee. He was a church leader and teacher of the Gospel in China—an extremely dangerous mission during that time. Watchman Nee established churches throughout China, preached the Gospel beginning at the age of seventeen, and held conferences to train Bible students and church workers. After the Chinese Communist Revolution, he was arrested in 1952 and imprisoned for his faith. He spent the last twenty years of his life in prison. Nee authored numerous books expounding on the Gospel; my favorite of his, which everyone should read, is *The Normal Christian Life.* I highly recommend that his many works, if they are not already included, be added to every

Christian's personal library. Watchman Nee was a wonderful author and a courageous disciple of Christ who bravely stood against the Chinese Communist regime.

Two other Christian heroes who exhibited great courage in the face of unspeakable horror were Corrie Ten Boom and Dietrich Bonhoeffer. Both of these saints certainly earned their place in history as mighty heroes of the faith! Corrie Ten Boom survived a brutal Nazi concentration camp, after she and her family were arrested for hiding Jews from the Nazis. Her elderly father and younger sister both died in captivity. Ms. Ten Boom ministered the Gospel while imprisoned and continued to minister to millions of people after World War II. She was Dutch, born in the Netherlands, and immigrated to the United States in 1977. She was a great woman of faith who touched many lives. Ten Boom authored a number of bestselling Christian books. Her best-known book, titled *The Hiding Place*, is an autobiography, and I highly recommend that you read it.

Pastor Dietrich Bonhoeffer was a German pastor who also opposed Hitler, Nazism, and the Holocaust. He was arrested for conspiring against the Nazi regime and executed just before the liberation of the concentration camp where he was being held and the end of World War II. His last words were, "*This is the end, for me the beginning of life.*"[16] Bonhoeffer and Ten Boom were two Christian heroes who were brave enough to speak up and take action to try to defeat an evil regime. I'm grateful for their sacrifice, and for the sacrifices of other like-minded individuals who were willing to do the same.

A few other heroes of the faith with brief explanations of their contributions to Christianity are: Dwight L. Moody (American evangelist; publisher, founder of Moody Bible Institute); Samuel Morris (formerly Prince Kaboo of Liberia; evangelist; instrumental in helping missionaries decide to evangelize Africa); George Mueller (bilingual British evangelist; spoke three languages [English, French, and German]; ran an orphanage for over ten thousand children in England; established 117 schools for Christian education for more than 120,000 students); R.A. Torrey (American and international evangelist and teacher;

pastor, author of numerous books—one of my favorite writers); Smith Wigglesworth (British evangelist; his wife taught him to read; the only book he would read was the Bible; divine healings and people raised from the dead through his ministry); William Carey (British missionary to India; known as the father of modern missions; translated Bible into Bengali and other Indian languages); Adoniram Judson (American missionary to Burma for thirty-seven years; established numerous churches; led almost eight thousand people to Christ; spent many years translating the Bible into the Burmese language; survived a brutal Burmese prison camp); David Livingstone (Scottish missionary to Africa), Gladys Aylward (British missionary to China; revered by Chinese people; adopted orphans; her story is told in book and film); Hudson Taylor (British missionary to China for fifty-one years; founder of an international mission); Jonathan and Rosalind Goforth (Canadian missionaries to China); Amy Carmichael (Irish missionary to India for fifty-five years; founded mission and orphanage; rescued girls sold as temple prostitutes; prolific writer); Lottie Moon (American missionary to China for forty years); Nate Saint (American pilot and missionary; killed by Amazon tribe in Ecuador); Jim and Elizabeth Elliot (American missionaries to Ecuador; Jim killed by Amazon tribe; Elizabeth later led natives to Christ); Ed McCully, Roger Youderian, and Pete Fleming (missionaries killed with Saint and Elliot in Ecuador); Eric Linddell (Scottish Gold Medal runner and Christian missionary to China; his life is reflected in the movie *Chariots of Fire*); John Livingstone (American missionary to China for forty years); John and Betty Stam (American missionaries to China; martyred for their faith by Communist Chinese soldiers); Helen Roseveare (British missionary to Congo for twenty years; doctor; author); Darlene Rose (American missionary to Papua New Guinea for almost thirty years; survived Japanese prison camp during World War II); Mary Slessor (Scottish missionary to Nigeria; rescued twins abandoned in the bush—the birth of twins was considered a curse in Nigeria); Charles Spurgeon (called Prince of Preachers; authored several books; founded college and opposed slavery); William and Catherine Booth (Salvation Army founders); Charles Finney (American leader of Second Great

Awakening in United States; called for abolition of slavery; promoter of civil rights for blacks and women); Kathryn Kuhlman (American evangelist and author; dealt in the miraculous; held numerous healing crusades with notable miracles); Amy George (grew up under communist rule in Soviet Union; evangelist; married American and immigrated to United States; wrote autobiographical book, *Goodbye Is Not Forever*—a must-read!); Moishe (Royce) Rosen (Jewish convert to Christianity; founder of ministry called Jews for Jesus—largest Messianic Jewish organization in the world); Oral Roberts (American evangelist; faith healer; founder of Oral Roberts University); Rick Renner; wife, Denise; and sons, Paul, Philip, and Joel (American ministers of the Gospel in Moscow, Russia; international evangelists who deal in the miraculous; founders of several ministries to serve poor and homeless; missionaries to Latvia in 1991 before relocating to Moscow in 2000; established numerous churches and Bible school; founder of Christian television network in former USSR; author of numerous books; *Dressed to Kill* about spiritual warfare is a must-read for every Christian); Philip Renner (worship leader; started major worship movement in Russia and surrounding countries; author; international evangelist; ministry deals in the miraculous); Alexander and Lilit Gorelov (Russian Christians and directors of House of Mercy under Renner Ministries, ministering to homeless; foster parents to thirty abandoned and orphaned children in Moscow); Lon Solomon (former pastor of McLean Bible Church; Messianic Jewish evangelist; member of board for Jews for Jesus; author; founder of Jill's House for ministry to children with severe disabilities); Pat Robertson (founder of Christian Broadcasting Network (CBN), Regent University, and Operation Blessing; ministry provides food, shelter, clothing, medical services, and assistance in national emergencies and to those in need; host of *700 Club*; founder of original Christian Coalition; and co-founder of American Center for Law and Justice (ACLJ), operates in miraculous; prolific author and televangelist); Terry Meeuwsen (cohost of the *700 Club*; founder of Orphan's Promise—a ministry after my heart); Sid Roth (Messianic Jewish televangelist and author; ministry operates in miraculous; founder of ministries called *It's Supernatural* and

Middle Eastern TV); Marilyn Hickey (American evangelist and author; successful ministry to Muslims and deals in the miraculous); Rabbi Kirt Schnieder (Messianic Jewish evangelist; ministers worldwide; author); Reinhard Bonnke (German evangelist and missionary to Africa; ministered in the miraculous to millions); Heidi and Rolland Baker (American missionaries to Mozambique; authors; established several churches; cofounders of Iris Global ministry to provide food, health care, and other physical and spiritual needs to the poor); Michael Brown (Messianic Jewish pastor; evangelist; teacher; revivalist of Brownsville Revival fame; author of numerous books); John Kilpatrick (pastor; evangelist; revivalist of Brownsville Revival; author of several books), Paula White-Cain (evangelist and former pastor; author; chair of Evangelical Advisory Board to President Trump; host of *Paula White Today* show; dynamic Bible teacher); Darlene Bishop Driscoll (pastor, author; conference speaker; founder of Darlene Bishop Home for Life, a ministry to unwed teens, providing food, shelter, life skills, and job training; and Solid Rock Orphanage for Brazil); Leah Sharibu (abducted by terrorist group Boko Haram in Nigeria; still being held captive because she refuses to convert to Islam and deny her faith in Christ).

Another great Christian heroine who certainly deserves recognition is Sonya Carson, the mother of Ben and Curtis Carson. This wonderful lady of the faith refused to be a victim or allow her two sons to adopt a victim mentality. She was raised in foster homes, married at age thirteen, divorced when her sons were young so she became the head of a single-parent household, but she refused to give up and be dependent on the government. This marvelous woman worked as domestic help, and adopted a "Yes, I can" attitude, refusing to become a victim of her circumstances. While working for prosperous families, she observed what made them successful and decided to apply those lessons to her own family. Mrs. Carson noticed that successful people spent a lot more time reading books than watching television. So, she employed this concept in the lives of her sons, requiring them to read and write two book reports weekly. She did this although at the time, she was illiterate—illiterate, but not dumb. Sonya Carson was just the opposite; she was very smart and a wise, godly woman. In addition to teaching her sons the importance of education, she also instilled in her sons the truth that hard work pays off. She left a great legacy, two very successful sons—one (Curtis) an aeronautical engineer, and the other (Ben) a famous neurosurgeon and author. Her son, Ben Carson, also grew up to be a candidate for president of the United States and the U.S. Secretary of Housing and Urban Development. What a great Christian testimony and a wonderful mother! I admire this woman immensely and believe that perhaps she deserves the "Mother of the Century" award.

The littlest big hero of the Christian faith has to be undoubtedly Tyler Stallings of Maryland. Little Tyler at the age of four became concerned for homeless veterans and wanted to build homes for them. Since Tyler was a bit young to construct homes, with the assistance of his mother (Andrea Blackstone), he started a business called Kid Time Enterprises. He became the Honorary CEO of the company and immediately went to work to improve the lives of others. Tyler is the founder of the Give Back to Veterans Project and other projects to help the homeless. He also created a project donating books to youth to encourage reading and literacy. This young superhero is an entrepreneur and philanthropist. He also coauthored a book with his mother titled, *Tyler Goes Around the World.* He and his mother teach youth to be producers, not consumers. Tyler delivers hero packs filled with snacks and hygiene products to homeless veterans in Maryland and the Washington, D.C. area. This young boy (now eight years old) is a frequently sought-after motivational speaker at events. He also appeared on ABC's *Little Big Shots* with Steve Harvey at age six, and has received numerous civic and honorary awards. This little guy has done more in his short life to help the less fortunate than most people ever contribute in a hundred years! This makes Tyler Stallings my number-one choice of a Christian hero! By the way, Tyler wears a superhero cape—not unlike Superman—with a big *T* printed on it while delivering the veteran hero packs. He is greatly beloved by the homeless veterans in Baltimore, and he is also one of my favorite Christian heroes! What an impressive résumé Tyler has already acquired; this young guy was born for greatness!

Like many of our war heroes, numerous unnamed Christian warriors have also given their lives—not for their countries but to further the Gospel of the Lord Jesus Christ. Only a few of them are mentioned by name in this book. Many heroes have been martyred and continue to be martyred daily in various parts of the world; some are beheaded, others are burned alive, while some suffer other terrible atrocities for their faith in Christ. Some new Christian converts are murdered by their family members after denouncing false gods and becoming followers of the Lord Jesus Christ. Other brave heroes walk the lonely path of being ostracized and disowned by their families when they leave cults, false religions, or atheism to gain a relationship with Jesus Christ! This happened to William Murray III, the son of Madalyn Murray O'Hair; his family completely rejected him after he renounced atheism and became a minister of the Gospel.

Jesus tells us in Matthew 10:37a, "He who loves father or mother more than Me is not worthy of Me." Suffering persecution in this life and forsaking others for the sake of the Gospel are often recognized trademarks of true disciples of the Lord Jesus Christ.

Sometimes I hear people remark that perhaps the Lord will have mercy on people and credit faith to individuals who were brought up in false religions, because these folks are so sincere and have little chance of coming to faith in Christ. After all, many of these individuals have great dedication to and love for their false god—the rationale is that the Lord may credit faith to their account based on their sincerity. But this is unsound theology that's not based on Scripture. The Lord says that all people are without excuse who don't know Him. If William Murray, a former atheist, surrounded by atheism all of his life, defied all odds and came to faith in Jesus Christ—then what excuse can others have for not following Jesus?

Those defying all odds certainly must be considered heroes of the faith. There is something very special about people who leave false religions and suffer persecution and sometimes even risk death from family members or other radicalized individuals in order to gain a relationship with Christ Jesus. It takes a very special kind of person with an unusual kind of courage and fearless determination to face that kind of opposition.

Another thing that makes many Christian heroes special is the generational nature of their faith and ministries. This is true of families such as Billy Graham, Darlene Bishop, Pat Robertson, and Rick Renner—and many others. Truly these families must be greatly beloved and highly favored by God. One day when I was speaking to Philip Renner (Rick's son) on the phone, he allowed his two-year old daughter to also speak to me briefly. Philip asked her to tell me whom she loves. In her sweet two-year old voice, she told me that she loves Je-e-s-us! This totally melted my heart, as I'm sure it melted the heart of God as well. Philip and Ella's two young daughters are well on their way to becoming Christian heroines—as are Rick and Denise Renner's other six grandchildren.

Incidentally, many children receive Jesus as Savior at a very early age, some as young as age four. These children are truly exceptional! They understand the Gospel, and some can even quote scriptures and expound doctrine. Studies show that the majority of individuals become Christians between the ages of four to fourteen years old. This is a short window of opportunity to reach people for Christ, so we should be directing our efforts toward children—but at the same time not ignoring evangelism to adults. Many people receive a call from the Lord at a very early age to become pastors, evangelists, or missionaries; this call should be encouraged by parents and others.

I've provided here a very short list of Christian heroes. Again, there are literally millions of evangelists and missionaries who fit the definition of heroes—too many to discuss in this book. Also, the contributions of the heroes I have mentioned are far too numerous to list. I recommend doing your own research of the wonderful men and women of God who have made numerous sacrifices to fulfill the Great Commission of Jesus Christ.

I would also like to mention that some Christian heroes led meager lives for the benefit of furthering the Gospel, foregoing modern conveniences for the sake of others. Some of the early evangelists traveled by horseback for thousands of miles in inclement weather to share the Gospel with other people; they sometimes encountered ridicule and abuse, were pelted with rotten eggs, and spit upon by a hostile public. Others traveled deep into jungles to share the Good News of Christ with people who had been untouched by modern civilization, and some were murdered by the very people they were trying to evangelize. Some Christian heroes held large crusades and healing services for decades, resulting in the miraculous and leading millions of people to faith in Christ. Others worked tirelessly to promote the Christian faith and advance civil rights; still others took bold, courageous actions to help defeat Communism and Nazism, while advancing the Gospel. Christian heroes have made the greatest contributions to society, but they are one of the most underappreciated groups.

Unfortunately, many of our most-honored heroes have come under assault by radicals in our country in recent years. Our brave military troops, police officers, border patrol agents, conservative civil rights activists, peaceful youth demonstrators, Christians, and even ministers of the Gospel are verbally—and sometimes physically—attacked by the radical left. The left's definition of a hero contrasts sharply with that of conservatives. People participating in violent protests and civil disobedience, showing disrespect for the military, projecting hostility toward law enforcement, ignoring the rule of law, and dishonoring the American flag are individuals more likely to gain the approval and affirmation of the left in our country today than true American heroes. Other people whom liberal progressives define as heroes are rich elitists whose focus is primarily on themselves. With liberals, and particularly radical leftists, it's all about them and nobody else! They have little interest in honoring others; they're too busy despising conservatives and admiring themselves.

C H A P T E R   1 3

Shh! Silencing Conservatives

He who justifies the wicked, and he who condemns
the righteous, both of them alike are
an abomination to the LORD.

PROVERBS 17:15 NASB

Not only do radicals despise conservatives, they also want to silence them. They want to silence them in the media, on college campuses, in churches, on social media platforms, and in the government. Their desire is to shut down free speech; eliminate conservative voices and ideals; divorce themselves from traditional values; and get rid of God's Word. This is why media outlets, television, and news articles ridicule conservatives and try to debunk their values. Also, various social media sites block conservative viewpoints, using lame and invalid excuses to silence those with whom they disagree. Hostile social media police remain constantly vigilant to censor conservative expressions, while promoting radical views.

The big tech giants of social media supposedly monitor and control abusive language and fake news items on Twitter, Facebook, YouTube, and Google. But from a strictly Christian perspective, it appears they only monitor conservative accounts and often block or suspend individuals whose ideology doesn't match theirs. Then once there's loud protesting, a spokesperson will make an insincere apology and provide a lame excuse for suspending conservative accounts. Some conservative accounts are suspended for brief periods of time, while others are blocked for lengthy periods. Once all individuals enjoyed freedom of speech in our country, but now only liberals and the radical left have earned that right. I sincerely hope someday there will be other alternatives to Twitter, Facebook, YouTube, and Google—future companies that are run by conservatives who will allow everyone a voice.

The only exception to freedom of speech on media sites truly should be for abusive, ungodly, and threatening language. I've seen despicable comments directed toward conservatives of all stripes—ministers, politicians, actors, journalists, talk show hosts, and ordinary citizens. The comments are crude enough to make most demons blush! But the insufferable perpetrators of these obscene comments are rarely censored. No, it's conservative voices that receive that distinction and dishonor!

Free speech is under attack in our country, but only if you happen to be a conservative. Social media gurus essentially blacklist conservatives and attempt to suppress their voices. There was a time in the United States when people sought to blacklist *the bad guys,* but it now seems *the liberal police* of social media primarily target conservatives for blacklisting. And as I've indicated earlier, conservatives also have been signaled out by government agencies, such as the IRS and the Justice Department, to blacklist and silence their voices. Previously, our government targeted suspected communists or other dangerous groups for blacklisting, never conservatives.

In 1947, Congress opened investigations into the activities of Hollywood actors, actresses, directors, and screenwriters whom the government suspected of being communist or communist sympathizers. This resulted in people suspected of being bad guys being blacklisted, which meant these folks didn't get much work and their careers suffered greatly. (I'm not necessarily saying this was right; I'm simply stating what happened.) Today, it's far more common for good guys to get blacklisted in Hollywood for their conservative politics than for bad guys to be censored. In fact, if bag guys get punished at all, it's usually for sexual harassment or gross cases of sexual misconduct. True, some in Hollywood—both the good and bad guys—are responsible for torpedoing their own careers. These people get blacklisted due to their own poor judgment and delinquency, but liberals with power are guilty of sabotaging the careers of some conservatives in Hollywood strictly based on their social beliefs and political affiliation. So, if actors, actresses, and screenwriters are politically conservative, it's probably best not to share this information in Hollywood. In fact, it might be wise to heed the advice of Proverbs 21:23, "Watch your tongue and keep your mouth shut, and you will stay out of trouble" (NLT).

Radical politicians and other liberals are also known to blacklist conservative businesses, such as Home Depot, Chick-fil-A, and local bakeries, florist shops, or others who do not share their worldview. A decision by radical city council members to ban Chick-fil-A at the San Antonio airport has cost the city an enormous amount of money in legal fees, plus it denies folks the opportunity to eat chicken Monday through Saturday while traveling through the airport. This is wrong, and I sincerely hope the decision will be reversed by the federal government's discrimination lawsuit against the city. Some smaller businesses have been irrevocably damaged by similar actions. Countries and people used to boycott others for important issues such as human rights violations or not complying with treaties, but today individuals boycott businesses or even entire countries simply to force their ideology upon others.

I admit that I have boycotted a number of liberal businesses, TV networks, the Oscars and other awards shows, movie actors, newspapers, and other leftist publications, but I don't make a big political statement about it. They just don't get my money or my viewership. I will make a political statement concerning one company and other guilty parties, though, because of their total disregard for decency. I plan to boycott Universal Pictures (aka Universal Studios) and all actors, directors, producers, screenwriters, or anyone associated with the movie called *The Hunt*—and I hope all conservatives will join me. Supposedly Universal Studios has canceled the release of this horrific motion picture, but one conservative actor says he doesn't believe the movie release will be canceled indefinitely—only delayed. Anyone involved in the making or promoting of the movie needs to be boycotted for life! The trailer of the movie is so nauseating and disgustingly disgraceful that it makes one wonder how human beings could be so vile. The movie was born from the pits of hell by diabolically evil people. The movie is about radicals hunting "deplorable" Trump supporters and viciously killing them—that's not likely to incite violence against conservatives in America, right? Words are hardly adequate to describe the horrific content of this monstrous film. Look up every synonym for *deplorable* or *disgraceful,* and they all can be applied to this movie. It's truly unspeakable, too bad or horrific to be expressed in words! If business executives decide to release *The Hunt* and conservatives are killed as a result of it, I plan to sue the sick executives and their coconspirators.

Sick people in Hollywood not only delight in silencing conservatives, but they also evidently receive great pleasure in imagining conservatives being hunted down by psychos and being brutally killed or horribly maimed. These people have very evil, twisted, sick minds.

The silencing of conservative voices is also very prevalent on college campuses today, where conservative speakers are harassed and often not allowed to speak. Some speakers are disinvited, and others must be whisked away from angry crowds of intimidating student protestors. Also, the attempt to silence conservative government officials is on display daily. This is the basis for the pushback on President Trump and his administration. We cannot allow radicals to silence our voices; our voices are the only voices dispensing truth! We also can't let them distort the truth coming from the Trump administration. President Trump is a true friend of conservatives, but the ungodly criticism directed at him is atrocious. If godless radicals can stop him, they are on their way to silencing other conservative voices as well. Radicals are barbaric enemies of godly society. They're determined to defeat Trump, silence conservatives, and vanquish Christian values. This revolting mindset lays the ideal groundwork for Democrat congressional members approving and pushing the Equality Act so strenuously.

So, what could possibly be wrong with the Equality Act, and who would oppose *equality* anyway? It sounds good and innocent enough on the surface, but it's short on substance and long on deception. If one reads the fine print, it appears to be yet another attack on religious freedom. Radicals are very clever at deliberately devising subtle ways in which to disguise their ambush on Christianity. If their assault is subtle enough, it might escape public scrutiny and successfully fly by unnoticed. This is how we end up with undesirable legislation that negatively impacts religious liberty for years to come. Christian leaders are concerned that the Equality Act essentially will make the Religious Freedom Restoration Act (RFRA) of 1993 null and void. The Equality Act amends the Civil Rights Act of 1964 to cover not only race but gender identity, and it prohibits discrimination against gays, lesbians, bisexual, and transgender individuals. So far, so good. But the Equality Act goes much further. It also provides men identifying as women to use women's bathrooms and locker rooms without regard for females' safety. Biological male prisoners (transgenders) also would be housed with female prisoners—again, without regard for the safety of female inmates. In addition, the law would prohibit medical professionals, based on religious objections, from refusing to provide transgender drugs or perform transgender surgeries—and the list goes on. It's a radical bill concocted in the hearts and minds of far-left Democrats to try to deceive a sleepy Christian community.

This radical bill was passed by the Democrats in the United States House of Representatives, but it isn't expected to come up for a vote in the Senate anytime soon. Thank God for the GOP! The Democrats would like nothing more than to silence Christians by enacting laws that override religious liberties. Passage of the Equality Act would be a defeat for Christianity and a basic reversal of most of the Religious Freedom Restoration Act. The RFRA is an important piece of legislation that needs to remain intact. Believe it or not, it was introduced to Congress by

Senator (then Congressman) Chuck Schumer and signed into law by President Bill Clinton—a very unlikely duo for religious liberty! Can't see that happening today. The Equality Act is an attack on Christian beliefs, and the enactment of such a bill would have a harmful impact on the Christian community. Parts of the RFRA presumably would not be impacted, such as the protection of sacred religious and burial grounds of Native Americans. But essential portions of the RFRA law would be erased by the Equality Act, which would have very devastating consequences for Christian hospitals, businesses, churches, and schools.

Laws that affect our country in a meaningful and truly positive way are always opposed by left-wing radicals. President Trump announced a new policy in July 2019 tightening restrictions on asylum seekers—*amen!* Migrants must first seek asylum in one of the countries they've traveled through before getting to the U.S. border. Only if their application for asylum is denied by another country would they be considered for asylum in the United States. Also, President Trump previously implemented a policy called Migrant Protection Protocols—referred to as the "remain in Mexico" policy. Radicals naturally oppose these policies, claiming they are inhumane and that Trump is xenophobic. These people know they're lying, but they say these outlandish things anyway. Most asylum seekers have no legitimate claim to asylum. Migrants are drawn to the United States for economic reasons, and to all that free stuff the radical left promises them! The left opposes every decent piece of legislation proposed by the president and continually try to shut him down. It's a small wonder that anything ever gets done by Congress.

Radicals have lost the ability to reason, along with their sense of decency. They accuse President Trump of committing acts of racism and lawlessness even when the president is following the same policies of previous administrations. To prove my point, President Trump could take a previous Executive Order (EO) issued by President Obama, dust it off, and indicate he's issuing the EO, but radicals would go berserk—claiming he is racist, homophobic, xenophobic, and every other existing or imagined phobia. When it's pointed out to them that the Executive Order is the exact same EO previously issued by President Obama, they would claim the ink in the wording is darker, therefore making it racist and phobic. When it's clearly shown to be the document signed by President Obama, radicals would still claim it's an illusion or some kind of trick perpetuated by Trump and the Russians.

President Trump and his supporters are accused of being racists, plus we're charged with all kinds of phobias—many of which we didn't even know existed until radicals were elected to political office. Liberal media pundits—the radical left's mouthpieces—are quick to repeat talking points and pronounce judgment upon conservatives for all their fallaciously perceived phobias. I once heard a pundit denounce President Trump as xenophobic because he had the courage to strengthen asylum policies and deport illegal immigrants. While running through her nonsensical talking points, she claimed the law and the president's actions were clearly racist. Two FOX commentators pointed out that a few Irish families who had overstayed their visas also had been deported. The liberal pundit dismissed their comments and stuck to her robotic talking points; she wasn't going to allow truth to get in the way of mindless talking points. She obviously couldn't think beyond her liberal bias or the repetitive talking points. If she had been able to think for herself, she would have realized there are not a lot of Irish, Italian, German, Russian, Dutch, or Japanese immigrants overstaying their visas. Most of the visa violators and illegal immigrants stem from other countries in the world. This pundit, not unlike a programmed robot, clearly couldn't think for herself—or think beyond her indoctrinated talking points! It is thoughtless liberals like her who want to silence us.

It doesn't matter to radical progressives that illegals have had their day in court—which costs taxpayers millions of dollars each year—and have been ordered to leave the country. It doesn't concern them that these individuals are breaking the law. Activist judges also try to circumvent the law, claiming some imagined infraction on the side of liberalism. They frequently oppose President Trump's agenda of enforcing the law and making the United States a safer place for all of us—even safer for activist judges and other radicals. Somehow, they don't seem very thankful, though. They just want to shut down conservative voices and policies, and they don't care how many laws are broken by illegals or themselves in the process. Proverbs 28:4–5 says, "Those who forsake the law praise the wicked, but those who keep the law strive [contend] with them. Evil men do not understand justice, but those who seek the LORD understand all things" (NASB).

The ability to think rationally or apply reason is a major issue in our nation today. What's lacking is godly wisdom and understanding; this is why many people praise evil and oppose good. What our country and the Christian church need most is another great spiritual awakening such as those experienced earlier in our history. The first spiritual revival called the First Great Awakening happened in the thirteen colonies in the 1730s and lasted until 1740. The Second Great Awakening occurred in the United States between 1790 and 1840. There also have been other regional revivals in our country since these two major spiritual awakenings.

Oh, that the Lord would send a mighty spiritual revival, and that His presence would be felt in Washington, D.C., and all across the land. And that benign prayers and feeble Bible studies currently offered by the United States Congress would be replaced by a heartfelt love for God. Wouldn't it be remarkable to have a Congress governed by God-fearing believers following the Word of God for direction, and a country where there is no longer an attempt to silence conservative voices or depose our beloved president? Now, that would truly make America great again, and keep it that way!

CHAPTER 14

A Great Spiritual Awakening

If my people, which are called by my name,
shall humble themselves, and pray, and seek my face, and
turn from their wicked ways; then will I hear from heaven,
and will forgive their sin, and will heal their land.

2 Chronicles 7:14 KJV

Wouldn't it be wonderful if the members of Congress had a great spiritual awakening; repented of their cut-throat ways; became born-again believers; resorted to reasonable, civil discourse; and served their constituents as uncompensated volunteers for one or two terms—and then left public service no wealthier than when they came? Also, wouldn't it be great if there were no corrupt lobbyists bribing greedy politicians? And wouldn't it be remarkable if journalists became Christian conservatives who reported the news honestly, with no more fake stories telecasting a gun range in Kentucky as intense fighting against Kurds in Syria, or broadcasting lies about a Catholic youth harassing a minority—stories intended to hurt President Trump politically and taint his foreign policy record, and malign the character of Christians?

How incredible it would be if activist judges, snobbish elites, supercilious Hollywood stars, and other ungodly radicals humbled themselves, denounced evil, and were converted to Christ. But none of this is likely to happen unless Christians first repent for their own rebellion and pray for renewal in our nation. A spiritual awakening is unlikely to touch the halls of Congress or other sinners until the hearts and minds of God's people are touched and cleansed by the Holy Spirit.

There must be a spiritual awakening within the Christian ranks before our prayers can truly impact the lives of sinners and the state of our union. The State of the Union address by the president tells us what is happening in the country economically and politically, but it doesn't reveal much about what is going on in the nation spiritually. God's State of the Union is a call for people to wake up spiritually, consider their ways, and repent!

We live in such a godless, broken society; sadly, apart from a major spiritual awakening in the United States and around the world, millions of people in our country and billions of individuals around the world will perish without a saving knowledge of Jesus Christ. A genuine spiritual awakening is the only hope for our country and other nations. If U.S. citizens don't awaken soon and abandon radical ideology, our country will become even more broken morally—and eventually become a godless socialist nation. The United States of America will become yet just another mismanaged country, like Venezuela, doomed to utter failure. If our country becomes a fatality from internal strife and immorality, irresponsible people will have only themselves to blame for the country's demise.

To their detriment and the detriment of the country, many reckless individuals—including unstable Christians—foolishly embrace socialism. Christians desperately need to repent and be resuscitated spiritually. Some listen to radical ideologues, but no one can listen to liberalism for very long without it infecting their thinking. They've allowed radical concepts to pollute their thinking and slowly change their worldview. This is why the Bible aptly instructs us to renew our minds *daily* to the Word of God, but some Christians are renewing their minds to the word of radicals who motivate them to help dismantle the foundations of our culture. Psalm 11:3 warns, "If the foundations are destroyed, what can the righteous do?" It's particularly sad and egregious when the righteous help to create havoc and foolishly participate in the dismantling of the nation!

Christians, in particular, need to learn how to better discern truth from fiction. God's way of doing things is the complete opposite than that of the secular world. It should be conspicuously clear that individuals whom godless people oppose and viciously attack are the people of whom God approves. And individuals upon whom radicals put their seal of approval are the people whom God opposes. This same concept also applies to things: Anything radicals put their stamp of approval on is what is rejected and opposed by God—and what they oppose is what God approves. All genuine Christians should understand this simple truth; this is Basic Christianity 101!

It should be clear to *all* Christians that they should support President Trump and his conservative agenda and reject radical politics. The Lord has made this so unambiguous that only deceived or rebellious Christians can possibly miss it! Christians should support President Trump, if for no other reason that his foreign policy stance, particularly relating to Israel, and his appointment of conservative judges and justices align with God's Word. No doubt God approves of Trump's strategy and friendship with the state of Israel.

President Trump has a very high approval rating among Israelis. Israel has even named a housing settlement in the Golan Heights after our president: Trump Heights. Israeli officials also are considering naming other sites in honor of President Trump. This type of recognition is a distinct honor for our president and the United States.

Most Israelis are well-informed about American politics because they realize that a more peaceful existence depends upon conservatives being elected to office in the United States. Our existence as a free and prosperous nation also depends upon citizens of the United States recognizing the dangers of radical liberalism and comprehending the virtues of conservative policies.

Our political relationship with Israel faltered under the Obama administration, and it likely would grow even worse under the leadership of other progressive Democrats. Keep this in mind when casting your vote in 2020 and beyond. The Jews are still God's chosen people, and Jerusalem is still His chosen city. One day, Jesus will return to set up His earthly kingdom in His Holy City—Jerusalem. Someday *Yeshua* (Jesus) will return to honor His friends and punish His enemies. So, let's pray that the majority of people in United States, Israel, and other countries around the globe will undergo a *great awakening*, as never experienced before, and will be ready for the return of Christ. Until then, we need to be busy fulfilling the Great Commission (Matthew 28:19; Mark 16:15) and praying for the peace of Jerusalem (Psalm 122:6).

We also must remain vigilant to keep our country safe from those who want to abolish the Gospel and diminish our standing in the world. In order to successfully fulfill the Great Commission, we must continue to exist as a free people and a prosperous nation. The best way to remain free, first and foremost, is to know the Lord Jesus Christ, and then vote to stay free. Don't vote for radical candidates who want to take us places we don't want to go. A majority of Democrats now view socialism favorably, even though socialism hasn't worked for any country in the past, doesn't work currently, won't work in the future, and certainly won't work for the United States of America. To remain free, we must vote for Trump and other like-minded candidates. Never vote for radical Democrats ever—period. And don't vote for liberal Republicans, unless there's no other alternative. All Christians should already know this; it's basic Christianity 101!

President Trump is on a mission to save our country from radicals and preserve our American way of life. He stands courageously against liberalism daily, and he deserves our utmost respect and our loyal support. Be wise; stay vigilant; and don't be swayed by liberal lies. If you love God, love our country, love your family, and value the American Dream, then support Trump and elect conservatives to political office. Democrats and socialism will take us down a road that we'll later regret traveling, and by then it'll be too late to salvage our country. The American Dream will be lost forever!

President Trump is doing a great job, in spite of what radicals say. He is the best president we have had since Abraham Lincoln, and like Honest Abe, he is fighting for freedom for all people and for the survival of our nation. Trump's most faithful supporters recognize this; that's why we love him. Only radical Democrats, RINOs, and their followers won't accept this conspicuous fact. He's fighting for their freedom too. They're just too obnoxious and deceived to realize it. What many of them don't understand is that under socialism the country would collapse. What they also fail to acknowledge is that the destruction of our country won't just affect conservatives, but it will adversely impact them too. We all live in this country together, so we'll either sink or swim together. This is something radicals don't seem to understand; evidently, they think they can sink conservatives, but somehow, they'll survive disaster and remain afloat.

These misguided individuals hate the United States, see it as an abhorrent evil, so they want to destroy and remake it. But this idea is absolute insanity perpetrated by foolish individuals. Only a great spiritual awakening and the election of wise, patriotic leaders will save our nation from the destruction perpetrated by the foolishness of radicals.

CHAPTER 15

The Word versus Empty Words

See to it that no one takes you captive through philosophy
and empty deception, according to the tradition of men,
according to the elementary principles of the world,
rather than according to Christ.

COLOSSIANS 2:8 NASB

Some of us are passionate about saving our country and seeing our fellow citizens renounce ungodliness and come to the knowledge of the Lord Jesus Christ. This is why we urge people to stop listening to and voting for politicians on the left. Many voters have been taken captive by radical philosophy and are being led by fanatics down a dangerous path that will result in a ditch of disappointment and ultimately disaster.

It's the sincere hope of conservative Christians that people wake up, abandon the broad way that leads to destruction, and enter the narrow gate that leads to safety and eternal life (see Matthew 7:13–14). Only deceived or ungodly people are foolish enough to remain on a road leading to destruction—when God offers the way to safety.

We are warned in Colossians 2:8 not to be taken captive by meaningless philosophy and senseless deception. We are to reject empty, foolish words and embrace *the Word*—the Lord Jesus Christ. Yet many people have become ensnared by preposterous indoctrination. Illogical ideology permeates almost every area of our lives—education, government, entertainment, and the media; unwary individuals inattentively have allowed irrational nonsense to infiltrate their minds and overpower their thinking. We must pray for these people to become enlightened and delivered by the power of the Word of God.

Several years ago, I heard someone ask Nancy Pelosi what her favorite *word* was. To my surprise, Ms. Pelosi responded that her favorite word was "*the Word.*" I'm not sure if she meant the Word of God contained in the Bible or *the Word* (meaning the Lord Jesus Christ). I assume she meant the Bible. If she reads the Word of God, she clearly doesn't understand it, based on her liberal ideology. I'm not the Salvation Police, but if Pelosi meant *the Word* (Jesus)—then it appears she doesn't understand Christ, either. Speaker Pelosi's radical theology conflicts with *both* the Word of God and the Lord Jesus Christ. A person cannot claim to love and follow Christ and the Bible, and at the same time contradict His Word and teachings without openly resisting and refusing to comply with God's standards. Individuals who know *the Word* personally, generally exhibit a fondness for the Lord and accept His values. Those opposing God's laws obviously don't know *the Word*, and they clearly are deceiving themselves when they claim to know Jesus Christ.

Many folks in the United States are committed to ritualistic religion, while others are relying on good works to get them into heaven. But religion nor good deeds are the way to eternal life. Neither good behavior, nor philanthropy, nor commitment to a false religion or even a Christian religion will earn an individual a home in heaven. Only a genuine relationship with Jesus Christ by being born again by the Spirit of God guarantees entrance into heaven.

Most people, many of whom attend church regularly, are trusting in their own righteousness instead of accepting the Lord's robe of righteousness. They're like the man identified in the *wedding feast parable* told in the gospel of Matthew chapter 22. In this story the king (Jesus) asks His servants to invite people to the wedding feast, but those invited will not accept the wedding invitation; instead, they ridicule and kill His servants. He sends out other servants to invite even more people to the feast, and the wedding hall is finally filled with guests. But when the King comes to greet the guests, He sees a man there who doesn't have on a wedding garment. The man without the proper wedding garment (who is clothed in his own self-righteousness) is thrown out of the wedding hall. In other words, this man came when he was invited, but he responded to the Gospel invitation based solely on his own terms. He came to church when he was invited, but he never accepted Jesus as his Savior—he was deceiving himself. This is why the apostle Paul warns in 2 Corinthians 13:5, "Examine yourselves to see whether you are in the faith; test yourselves. Do you not realize that Christ Jesus is in you—unless, of course, you fail the test?" (NIV). Paul also provides an additional warning in James 1:22, "Be doers of the word, and not hearers only, deceiving yourselves." Further, the Bible states in Romans 8:16, "The Spirit Himself bears witness with our spirit that we are children of God." I call these three scriptures and others the *salvation test.*

Over and over again, various scriptures tell us how to ensure that we are in the faith, that we are born-again believers and future citizens of heaven. It's of the utmost importance for people to know with certainty that they have a saving faith and are true believers in Christ. I suspect there are many individuals today, especially in the United States, claiming to be Christians but are actually deceiving themselves. This is why God cautions us repeatedly in His Word about lying to ourselves, and He shows us how to ascertain that we actually know Christ. The Lord doesn't want anyone to perish without a saving relationship with Jesus Christ, but He desires that all people repent and be saved. (See 2 Peter 3:9.)

If people are unsure of their eternal destination, they should repent of their sins and ask the Lord Jesus Christ to guide their lives. After a person repents, it's important for them to read the Bible. If a new convert is Jewish, I recommend they begin reading the Book of Matthew in the New Testament. If a new convert is a

Gentile (someone who is not Jewish), they should begin by reading the Book of John in the New Testament. Both Jews and Gentiles may want to read the Books of Psalms and Proverbs as they're reading the rest of the New Testament. After growing in faith, I recommend that they read the rest of the Old Testament, then continue reading through the entire Bible annually while studying the Scriptures in depth. It's also important to attend a true Christian church, share your faith with others, renounce your old lifestyle, and live by God's laws and godly agenda.

Knowing Christ and becoming a Christian is the most important decision anyone will ever make. In addition, finding and attending a church where the full Gospel is being preached is very important for growing in one's faith. Another important aspect of being a Christian is being politically active. I urge Christians to vote for conservative candidates who promote godly values, and to renounce empty deception, senseless words, and meaningless philosophies.

Again, people should determine without a doubt that they know the Lord Jesus Christ (*Yeshua*—the Jewish Messiah) as their Savior. Many individuals who are committed to false or ritualistic religions erroneously claim to know God. But the god they know is a false god, created in the imagination of man. It's relatively easy to recognize false religions. Many of them claim that Jesus is a pretty good guy, a good teacher, or perhaps a prophet, but they deny that Jesus is the Eternal God. Some false religions don't acknowledge Jesus at all in their teachings. One religion teaches that Jesus never claimed to be God, but nothing could be further from the truth. The Bible states Jesus is God, and Jesus Himself claimed on numerous occasions to be God—that's why the religious rulers frequently tried to stone or kill Him—and ultimately did crucify Him. Even in the story portraying the *rich young ruler* in the gospels of Matthew, Mark, and Luke, Jesus tried to get the rich ruler to recognize Him as God. Since man's knowledge is finite but God's understanding is infinite, people try to create a god in their image that they can understand. Often what individuals don't understand, they make concessions for and compromise their understanding of God.

Most false religions either reject Jesus totally or claim that He is a lesser god or a created being, but not the Eternal God identified in the Christian Bible. To explain Jesus away, false prophets assert that an angel appeared to them, providing greater spiritual insight and a better understanding of God—and *poof!*—Jesus either magically disappears or is reduced to a trivial god or an insignificant prophet. Of course, none of this meets the biblical tests in the Word of God. We are warned by the Lord in 1 John 4 to "test the spirits" to determine if they are from God. The Holy Spirit, our own spirit, and demonic spirits can all speak to us. We can experience the manifested presence of God, but demon spirits also can appear to us. This is the reason we must train our senses to discern the difference between good and evil (Hebrews 5:14).

False religions and false gods have been around essentially since the beginning of time. False religions are created by those who disagree with God's way, who desire to invent their own way to God or heaven. All false religions have their origin at the Tower of Babel. They all result from man's pride and rebellion. Some folks actually realize they have bought a false religion, but they are too prideful to leave it because they don't want to admit they're wrong. Sadly, some people even move from one false religion to another. Jesus Christ is *the way* and *the only way* to heaven—period! Individuals in false religions and other sinners should read the gospel of John for verification of this. Any true Christian translation of the Bible will confirm what I've stated. My favorite Bible translation is the New King James Version, but there are other good translations. Do not read the New World Translation, as it has been altered considerably and is published by a false religion. If you're in a false religion and desire to know the truth, please don't trade one false religion for another. Read the Bible for yourself, repent of your sins, and ask the Holy Spirit to guide you to a true Christian church—and watch Christian programming such as the *700 Club* and CBN News on the Christian Broadcasting Network and programs on the Trinity Broadcasting Network (TBN). Don't listen to liberal pastors who trash President Trump or promote liberalism; instead find conservative programming and locate a conservative church that doesn't succumb to political correctness. Steer clear of social justice churches and avoid pastors who encourage people to vote for radical Democrats.

If people will heed this advice, they will be able to avoid false religions and save themselves a multitude of problems. They also eventually will be able to train their senses to discern nonsensical philosophy by comparing it to the Word of God. Further, they'll be able to identify true Christian churches and godly pastors who preach the full Gospel and aren't afraid to expose the deceptive lies of radical ideology and the dangers of liberal theology. Again, dear sinner or new convert to Christ, avoid false religions, false doctrine, and liberal churches.

Liberal pastors cause confusion by encouraging people to remain loyal to the disastrous Democrat Party, while other pastors tell congregants it doesn't matter if Christians vote for radicals or conservatives—but it does matter in this life and in the one to come. These pastors are lying to their congregations. Not all pastors are Christians, and not all pastors are honest. They're being dishonest, because some are liberal Democrats and others are afraid of offending people in their congregations. Some pastors fear losing finances and church membership. My sister's pastors in Lebanon, Ohio, don't have this problem. They have no fear of offending folks or of making it clear where they stand on social or cultural issues. And if you've guessed already that they have lost a large chunk of their congregation, you wouldn't be wrong! My sister told me that during the Obama era, a large number of people, while listening to a fiery sermon about the ills of our society and ungodly politics, got up and exited the auditorium, never to return.

This also happened to the conservative church we are now attending in Albuquerque after the Trump victory. People left the church in droves because the pastor used wisdom and voted for President Trump. The church lost over 1,400 of its members, because they learned that their pastor had taken a stand for Christian principles; imagine that! This probably happens frequently in numerous Christian churches where the truth of the Gospel is preached, and where pastors aren't afraid to take a stand for righteousness. Undoubtedly, churches are stronger without the liberals and their ungodly theology tarnishing their congregations.

Again, if you want to know the Lord and have a stable relationship with Him, then avoid radical churches and pastors promoting liberalism and preaching social justice. All true Christian churches promote conservative values while trying to defeat radicalism. Beware of churches that don't. Throughout the eight years of President Obama's administration, liberal pastors were singing a love song—not to God, but to Obama. I believe the Lord has a word for pastors such as these—those preaching a social-justice gospel and those voting for radical Democrats. This word from the Lord can be found in Isaiah 56:10. The scripture reads, "His watchman are blind; they are all ignorant; they are all dumb dogs; they cannot bark, sleeping, lying down, loving to slumber." Fortunately, this scripture doesn't apply to the vast majority of ministers today. Most pastors are still good guys or gals who are dedicated to the Lord, the truth, and His standards, or at least I hope they are. Simply use wisdom choosing a pastor.

Many authors, writing a book such as this, often conclude with a sinner's prayer. I purposefully have chosen not to do that, but rather I encourage individuals to read the Word of God for themselves and repent of their sins as necessary. A prayer doesn't profit anyone unless it is prayed in sincerity; reciting a *sinner's prayer*—without repentance and no understanding of the Gospel message—is futile. There's nothing intrinsically wrong with a sinner's prayer, as long as it's properly administered and understood by those professing it. Individuals not grasping the full Gospel message and who aren't ready to accept Jesus Christ as their Savior will pray a meaningless prayer and walk away as lost as ever. Jesus said in John 3:3, "Most assuredly, I say to you, unless one is born again, he cannot see the kingdom of God." For individuals to be born again, they must confess their sins to God, repent of their sins, accept the sacrifice of Jesus for their sins, turn away from a sinful lifestyle, and live according to God's Word. Until people do this, their spirit is not born again. Praying the sinner's prayer without true repentance cheapens grace, and it is not true salvation. People generally don't get saved suddenly.

Salvation is a process. The light normally begins to dawn gently, and it continues to shine more brightly until the truth of the Gospel is fully understood and grasped by people.

May the Lord bless you for reading this book, and may your path be enlightened. My prayer is that you live your life in a manner that will help to dispel darkness and foster light, by following Jesus and pursuing His plan for your life.

ACKNOWLEDGMENTS

I want to take this opportunity to thank all those who helped with the writing of this book. First of all, I thank my Lord Jesus Christ for leading me to write my thoughts and many of His words of wisdom. I also want to thank my husband, Johnny, other family members, and friends for granting me the time to write. And I want to thank all the generals of the faith who have stood and who still stand in the gap for the United States of America. I particularly thank those who had the wisdom and foresight to discern early on how important the election of Donald J. Trump was for the survival of Christian liberty and for the health of our nation. I want to personally thank Liberty University President Jerry Falwell Jr.; Pastors Darrell Scott, Robert Jeffress, Paula White-Cain, and Evangelist Franklin Graham. And I give a shout-out to all members of the Christian community and prayer warriors who tirelessly stood—against stiff opposition—to support God's choice in the 2016 presidential election. Keep up the good work, and let's ensure that President Trump is reelected in 2020, along with a whole host of other conservative candidates!

There are many people to whom I am grateful for their continuing prayers and encouragement. I'm especially indebted to and thankful for Philip Renner, who encouraged me and prayed for me during the long process of writing and publishing this book. I am also grateful for two of my good friends (Sandie Johnson of Albuquerque, New Mexico, and Rose Logan of San Antonio, Texas) for their loving support and earnest prayers of encouragement.

A heartfelt thanks is extended to my amazing publisher, Keith Provance, *Word and Spirit Publishing*, and my skillful editor, Christy Phillippe, to whom I owe a great debt of gratitude. And I sincerely thank President Donald Trump and his family, who helped inspire me to write this book. I also thank all the readers who purchased the book; may you be immensely blessed by its contents.

NOTES

INTRODUCTION

1. Quote by Frank Haley, *Coffee and Conversation,* TV program aired on KCHF, Albuquerque, New Mexico, February 12, 2020.

2. Crosswalk.com, "20 Influential Quotes by Dietrich Bonhoeffer," from *20 Inspiring Dietrich Bonhoeffer Quotes,* Emily Maust Wood, November 23, 2015.

CHAPTER 3

3. https//en.wikiquote.org/wiki/Jerry_Falwell.

4. https//www.brainyquote.com/authors/albert_einstein_quotes.

5. https//en.wikipedia.org/wiki/Rules-for-Radicals.

6. https//en.wikipedia.org/wiki/Rules-for-Radicals.

7. https//en.wikipedia.org/wiki/Rules-for-Radicals.

(Notes 5 through 7 are partial quotes from Saul D. Alinsky's book entitled *Rules for Radicals,* 1971.)

CHAPTER 8

8. Twitter, Les Dunaway tweet, "San Francisco: Where dogs step in human poop."

CHAPTER 10

9. https//en.wikipedia.org/wiki/Engel_v_Vitale.

CHAPTER 12

10. https//en.wikiquote.org/wiki/Nathan_Hale.

11. https//www.goodreads.com/quotes/267811-no-soldier-ever-really-survives-a-war.

12. https//myhero.com/A_Murphy_dnhs_US_2012_ul.

13. https//www.usatoday.com/story/news/2018/08/22/trump-awards-john-chapman-congressional-medal-honor/1060626002/.

14. https//www.veteransunited.com/network/paul-smith-soldiers-stand-against-the-enemy-with-a-50-caliber.

15. https//www.christianquotes.info/quotes-by-author/billy-graham-quotes/.

16. https//en.wikipedia.org/wiki/Dietrich_Bonhoeffer. (See note 44, Bethge, Eberhard. *Dietrich Bonhoeffer: A Biography;* 927.)

Note: Much of the information about heroes included in chapter 12 was obtained from researching biographies on Wikipedia.